I Hate Porta-Potties, Sprinkles and
Tight Underwear

I Hate Porta-Potties, Sprinkles and Tight Underwear

Enjoy!

Hoover

Emily Joanne Hoover

Kissy, Kissy Kiss Ups!

Kiss ups to my family, especially my dear sweet Hubby who has put up with a lot of book clutter. Okay, a lot of other clutter too as my focus, such as it is, has been on finishing this book. If you could see the frown lines on his forehead you might guess life with me isn't always easy. (I don't call myself "bitch" for nothing.)

Thanks to my fun fans and friends who have supported me. Thanks to our two sons, who allowed me to include some of their writing.

Thanks also to our only grandson, who has been very supportive.

Special kissy, kissy, kiss ups to my very loyal friend and typist, Leslie Rahberg, who has typed, and retyped it again. I would like to thank the following special friends for their help: Cathy Garry, Elsie Keller, Emily Carmain, Julia Soukup and editing by my son T.J. Hoover. A special thank-you to Sherrie Steele for finalizing my cover design, and formatting the book for the publisher, and for her graphic work and advice. Gratitude goes to Judy Stroup for her continuing support. There are many others who have spurred me on and will live in my heart forever. You know who you are. Thanks also to the members of the Florida Writers who have inspired and encouraged me.

Comments from Loyal Readers

"This is a book about life written by an up-beat lady (well, maybe not the lady part since she calls herself "The Bitch"). Emily tells us how to keep our spirits up no matter what the circumstances. Her great one-liners are sure to have you laughing out loud. Emily writes from the heart and includes touching moments as well as good advice. Emily shares her life hoping to put a smile on the faces of her readers thereby enhancing their lives even if it's just for the moment." - *M. A. Bator*

"Your book was a delight to read... I read it yesterday afternoon and last evening, laughing all the way to the end. Wonderful philosophy in many places, especially page 99, the 5th & 6th paragraphs. Loved the line about getting ice cream at the crematory on page 147. Speaking of laughter, take a look at page 53 and the name Isaac, the son of Abraham and Sarah. In Hebrew, the name Isaac (Yitzchak) means laughter, i.e., mockery. God has a keen sense of humor. Thanks again." - *L. Leckie*

"What a delightful hoot!!! Enjoy her drive through the days of her life and days of her families' lives..." - *A Florida Reader*

"You can pick this book up and read any chapter, and it will have you laughing until you put it down. Fun and easy to read, this book takes you on a hilarious trip through life, and teaches you not to take yourself so seriously. We loved it!" - *A Supporter*

"I was visiting a book store on a recent vacation and the author was present promoting this book. I purchased the book and was laughing out loud on the plane back home! The book consists of many mini-stories and is a hoot! While I was reading the book, I could picture myself in similar situations and that just made it all the funnier. That vacation destination is now my home and just this past weekend was again visiting the bookstore and ran into the author. We chatted for about fifteen minutes and when I left, my jaws were tight from laughing so much. This book is as funny as the author is in person! Give yourself some comic relief and pick up a copy of this book. It's a book you'll enjoy and will want to share with others. I'm purchasing several copies to share with girlfriends over the holidays!" - *A Southern Fan*

"I gave this as a gift to another great lady. She loved it! It arrived in brand-spanking new condition as promised."   - *Barbara Regen*

"Emily is a hoot! Emily has a unique sense of humor and I loved her book! I really did laugh out loud more than once." - *Kathy*

Contents

Chapter 1 *Fun With Artsy Fartsy People*

Love those people one and all! This group includes all kinds of creative artists, those who paint, write books, sing, play instruments, etc. What a fun imaginative group! Most of these folks have wonderful senses of humor.

Sometime ago a guy friend was giving a painting demo to our North Carolina artist group. He told us a kind of longwinded story about how he doesn't make up stuff but paints from real objects. He showed us several of his contemporary paintings, explaining that the backyard view would have drawn the viewer to look there instead of at the rest of the painting, thus he painted a brick wall there. Sorry, I couldn't help myself when I said, "So much for painting what is in front of you." He grinned. Later on he demonstrated a painting of a previously drawn pear. I asked where the pear was. He said, "I was going to bring it but I got hungry and ate it." "So much for painting from real life," I said. He laughed along with our friends. What a talented sweet guy. He has done so much for our small mountain group. He knows we all love him!

A member of our Florida art group was giving a program. She thanked us for the opportunity. She went on to say that we were such a nice group of people to invite her. I said, "That's because you don't know us." She laughed, relaxed and gave an awesome presentation.

I also love my creative writer friends. Most of them love to book sign with me because we have fun and I help sell their books. In fact, I received a recent e-mail from Bruce Thomason, former Jacksonville Beach police chief friend, who thanked me for helping him sell books at a recent book signing.

Bruce is the author of *Blood Toll*, *The Six O'clock Rule* and *Perception of Power*; I have purchased four or five books from him for friends and family. Frankly, I haven't and am not going to read his book as I am not into crime stories. I hear he is a good writer. I told him I want to be a bank robber in one of his books. I feel it is only fair he does this as I have mentioned him in two of my books. I love this guy; he is like a brother. He and his cute wife and I hope to hang out together again at the Florida Writers Annual Conference in October.

We have a local writers group that is full of creative fun people. We try to support each other in every way we can. It is nice to be a part of these art and writing groups as creative ventures are not easy. We appreciate the constructive advice and support given.

Maybe I love the artsy fartsy folks so much because, like my Dalmatian friends, they "get my humor."

Speaking of artsy fartsy, what about Maxine? She is a comic-book type character created by Hallmark designer John M. Wagner. He says Maxine is a cross between several relatives, aunts and his grandmother. Maxine was first seen on funny sarcastic Hallmark cards starting in 1986. I don't want to have blue hair like Maxine or the women I saw in church years ago. As long as Hubby can afford it — and I can sit in a beauty salon chair — I will be a blonde. I am sassy and at times have Maxine type moments, okay?

Over the last fifteen years I have received multiple "Maxine" books. Maxine, according to "People" magazine is the "Mother lode of laughs." That comparison to me is fine and dandy. What really gets me is the crotchety crabby Maxine. I hope I am not like that lady! I try to be bad in a good way. By that I mean in a funny bad way, okay?

Sometime ago I asked two of my best friends, "Am I really cranky like Maxine?" One said, "No, but you do have fast retorts similar to Maxine." My friend Cheryl said she thought I have a funny attitude like Maxine. I know I have fun giving people — usually guys — a rough time. Okay, from time to time I do gripe to close girlfriends about life's problems. Don't we all? I'll say I can relate to Maxine's love of chocolate over chicken soup. Maxine loves her old robe; so do I! Maxine has an attitude! I hear I have one too. Surprise, surprise, surprise! The artist who draws Maxine, John Wagner, went to art school. I wish I had taken more art classes at The Ohio State University (OSU). John has a team of writers, I wish I did. My favorite John Wagner line (or from his team) is, "It's nice to see you doing so well at your age... You know breathing is everything." Crazy but true and oh, so funny. Love it!

Maxine, I have to tell you, hasn't aged since 1986. How can that be? Frankly if you had work done, you didn't get your money's worth. Did Joan Rivers overspend? Maxine, maybe I am a bit like you. I admit to being older than some or most, depending upon where I am. I am blonde by choice. Maxine, you keep your hair blue. You are short and not attractive. At least I am taller and in 1986, I looked better than you. I HATE bras. Bet you do too. Hey, girlfriend, you know you're getting old when you can't wait to get home to get the damn thing off. Maxine and I share our love of big glasses. I feel they help cover up my face – always good. The other type of big glasses give you more to drink.

Margaritas, anyone? Any glass half full needs to be FULL, right?

Maxine, I guess you have figured it out that becoming older isn't all bad. Less hair means it dries faster. Most people don't expect as much from older folks – mentally or physically.

This means anyone could hit you below the belt before you know what is going on, if you understand me.

One big advantage of old age is we can always entertain ourselves by counting our too-visible blue veins. Another plus is we don't have to remember your name or anyone else's. Guess what? We have outlived many of our earlier competition and watch out, we might outlive you. You do know fun and funny people live longer. Life is up to you. It's all about believing in God and having a grateful happy life. You can do it too!   P.S. Maxine, I challenge you to come to life so we could hang out together.

Chapter 2 *Fun With Making People Laugh*

It's fun! Yes, it is fun, fun, fun making people laugh! Frankly, I'll do about anything to get someone to laugh – especially guys. Usually by insulting guys in some way. (Remember, I am a female version of Don Rickles.) For instance, a guy may hold a door open for me, and I say, "Thank you so much!" They say, "You're welcome." Then I turn and say, "Who would believe you are so nice, just looking at you." They grin or if I'm lucky, laugh. People that overhear me will laugh too. When joking around with guys I often ask them how old they are; then I tell them they look older. Not sure why I get away with this stuff, but I think it is because I generally like people. I believe it shows in my smile and vocal tones. A guy may act like he is insulted, but apparently he really isn't as he soon will start a conversation with me.

Some gals think they are hot, some think they are not. Some think they are smart, some know they are not. Some women think they are beautiful, some know they are not. But, cookie, I am not short. I know I am a smartass and obnoxious.

I know that I am not a beauty but I have more fun than most people my age and perhaps more friends. Today, if a person is insulting another, it had better be a joke.

Why some people are funny and others are are not? Most comedians started being funny to get others to like them or to get attention. Then somewhere along the line they get addicted to laughter. It produces endorphins that feel good – no, really good!

Some comedians have had a real hard time in life. Some have had real mental health issues, as well. An example is Robin Williams; in addition he had drug abuse problems, which didn't help. What a loss!

There are all kinds of comedians, young and old, attractive and unattractive. There are those that aren't nearly as funny as they think they are. Some have a dry wit, other produce belly laughs, some giggles, some re-do old jokes, but most of today's comedians write funny stuff about their lives or make funny comments about current or topical issues. Other comedians turn simple observations into really funny stuff. Regardless, doing stand-up is tough. You have to start with a bang, have jokes that link well with others, then a bang-up ending. Your set is most often five minutes. As time goes on you may be asked to do twenty or thirty minutes.
When you are in front of an audience that can be a really long, long, long time.

It is much harder doing stand-up than most think. If you want to give it a try, call your local comedy club and ask when amateur night is scheduled. Go and watch others before you try out. You may get some ideas from watching "Last Comic Standing" on NBC. There are a lot of do-it-yourself books out there to help you learn to write your own material.

If you want to become a comedian or write "funny stuff," you should take a comedy class if at all possible. You try your funny stuff out on friends or even strangers you encounter in your life. You bring in a joke in the middle of conversation. Timing of place and time is important. The pacing of your material and the inflection of your voice are both to be considered in timing. I prefer to use every day funny stories I hear, of funny stuff that happens to me or because of me. Humor needs to be current or it won't remain funny. One big thing to remember is – you usually have to surprise people in order to get a joke or story to work, or be shocking or insulting. Sweet doesn't work.

You also have to have very thick skin. I was once booed off a stage at a black club in Atlanta, Georgia. I was getting laughs but the MC cut my mike. He did it to other comedians, too. I later heard he had drug issues or maybe it was envy, who knows. It never happened before or since. Lack of laughter isn't good. You can also get drunks in the audience that think they are suddenly funnier than you. I have found in my life some people criticize others when they have a low self-worth. In other words, it makes them feel better when they put someone else down. These people are often hecklers in an audience.

You might find the following books helpful: Jon Macks' *How to Be Funny: The One and Only Practical Guide for Every Occasion, Situation and Disaster (No Kidding)*, New York, Simon and Schuster, 2013, paperbacks. Jon Macks was a comedy writer for Jay Leno, Steve Martin, Billy Crystal and Whoopi Goldberg. Another source is Gene Perret's *Comedy Writing Step by Step*, New York, Samuel French, Inc. 1960. Gene Perret was the head writer for Bob Hope and he also has written for Carol Burnett, Phyllis Diller and Bill Cosby.

Chapter 3 *Fun At a Grand Wedding*

Recently our family was invited to a big Italian wedding held in Key West, Florida. The bride's family came from Italy and Canada to take part in the special wedding festivities. (The bride has dual citizenship in those countries.)

The wedding rehearsal was Friday afternoon and followed by an informal party. This included a number of drink options, and a hearty buffet of hors d'oeuvres with live music and a lot of Italians. The wine flowed. People drank and let's say talked, ate, drank, and talked some more as the very pleasant music was played. This fun event was held outside at the Conch Restaurant on their patio in Key West. The weather was pleasant, thank God, as it had rained the evening before. I wouldn't have been surprised if the Italian contingent showed up in a long line of Fiats. You may have seen the TV commercial that starts with, "The Italians are coming." Our new Italian friends all spoke English – most very well. We met a lot of these fun attractive people with delightful personalities. They reminded me of the Kardashian clan, one better looking than the next. I just am not normally in the shadow of so many good-looking people even though my family isn't bad-looking.

Saturday morning before the wedding my family went to see The Harry Truman Little White House and then to lunch. Soon it was time to dress for the wedding. Photos were taken in the garden facing the ocean of The Casa Marina, the famous old Flagler Hotel. Fans, listen up! I hate, hate, hate having my photo taken but how can you say no to a beautiful bride and groom you love? After everyone had been photographed several times, we all boarded the small open-seated motorized Conch Train and were driven to the church.

This Episcopal Church is said to be the oldest non-Catholic church in Florida. It's on a large lot, landscaped with all kinds of beautiful tropical plants and wonderful stained glass windows. I have never been to such a joyous ceremony. Often I get weepy at weddings. What can I say? My grandson looked so special in his custom-made tux that his loving in-laws had made for him. He is six foot two, attractive with blue eyes and strawberry blond hair. He wears a size forty-two tall (perfect model size, I hear.) His tux fit him like a glove with the perfect white shirt and cuff links. His new Italian black leather shoes completed "the hunk look." Honestly, he looked as good as any Hollywood star. (I told him he would never look that good again.) Ha ha.

I noticed his eyes light up as he viewed his bride coming down the aisle. I tried to contain my tears as I looked from the bride to the groom. My grandson was getting red. I thought, he's in trouble, as his eyes filled with tears. By the time his bride got to the altar he was wiping them away. She grabbed his hand and before he knew what was happening, she planted a kiss on him. Soon they were both beaming – sweet – sweet – sweet and yes, unexpected. We all giggled. The bride wore her shoulder-length curly hair pulled back topped by a long, lovely lace veil. Her dress was white strapless. It was sophisticated handmade lace with train. Her maid of honor, the bride's sister, wore a dress made of a heavy lime green satin. It had a fitted bodice, short sleeves with an off-the-shoulder design with a contrasting waist cummerbund. It was knee-length and she looked wonderful. The junior bridesmaids, about eight to eleven years old, were cousins of the bride. Their dresses were of the same design. They looked adorable! The mother of the bride wore a similar long dress in a dusty rose silk and I believe one of the loveliest "mother of the bride dresses" I have ever seen. The guys all looked terrific in their tuxes.

The beautiful wedding couple held hands and were mostly solemn during the vows. The priest had gone to school with the groom's father. The bride's sister and the groom's father, also a priest, each read a meaningful passage from the Bible. The very talented organist, a friend of the couple, traveled from Fort Lauderdale to be a part of this special ceremony.

After the church bells rang, all the guests boarded the tram to be driven to the Casa Marina for the champagne, wine or drinks and fun before dinner. What is a glorious dinner? This was their menu:

- Menu –

FIRST COURSE
Pan Seared Jumbo
Scallop with
Roasted Tomato,
Artichoke and Fennel Salad with Micro Greens

SECOND COURSE
Spinach Crepe with Spinach and Ricotta Cheese,
Sun-dried Tomato, Pesto Sauces and Crispy Pancetta

MAIN COURSE
8oz. Tenderloin
Rubbed with Truffle Butter in a Burgundy Reduction with
Lemon

DESSERT
Wedding Cake and Assorted Desserts

The floral arrangements were exceptional! They consisted of hydrangeas, white tulips, white lilies, and white roses with touches of lime. The arrangements looked like they were in wine glasses on steroids at about twenty-seven inches tall. The floral stems were cut short and were mostly covered by white hydrangea blooms. We all agreed these were the most beautiful arrangements we had ever seen.

I'm not sure who planned the music but it was fun, fun, fun! My daughter-in-law told me it was the most awesome party she had ever been to. The parents gave toasts as did the father of the groom, the bride's sister and brother. They were humorous yet very loving. The bride and groom both gave tributes to each other's families and friends. Again the wine flowed. If you were not a wine drinker there were lots of other options.

But hey, most were Italian and thus lots of wine.

One of the Italians had been a friend of the bride's mother since 1971. Apparently she lost her husband just a few days before the wedding. They had been married a long time and were looking forward to the wedding in the U.S. so she had him cremated and still attended with her other friends. She knew that her husband would have wanted her to do so. She was this slender classy lady who was a beautiful dancer. I introduced myself and asked her if she had been or was a professional. She said yes, she was, and that she works teaching women to dance in order to "let go" of emotional baggage. In her black outfit with her short gray hair moving to the music, she was stunning!

Our widowed sister-in-law and her attorney daughter were attending the wedding from California, along with another daughter (an attorney for Nissan in Nashville). They stayed at Casa Marina. We stayed at Best Western. (Maybe it wasn't the "Best" in the west, but it was less pricey.) Key West is NOT a budget location, kids!

Even at our ages we aren't always wise. Doesn't near the airport mean something to you, Emily? Maybe noise from planes? Usually I carry an air filter with me to cut out outside noise and to help keep allergies at bay. Having forgotten mine, I borrowed a less effective one. It is always challenging to sleep away from home, isn't it?

I had spoken to the relatives about meeting up on Saturday to see some of Key West's sites. It didn't work out as Hubby and I didn't have our own "wheels." We had driven down to the wedding with our son, the father of the groom, and his partner of nearly twenty-five years. Long story short, we decided to see each other at the church and hang out at the wedding reception. But surprise, surprise, out of thousands of visitors in Key West, we ran into each other at Harry Truman's Little White House. Crazy, isn't it?

The wedding was so spiritual, beautiful and joyous; the wedding reception and party were beyond wonderful for everyone attending. Yet to me the events were even more special as the groom was my only grandchild, who I adore more than life itself. Folks, I couldn't have expected to find him a more perfect partner. After attending a small high school in Italy as teenagers, they met again ten years later. This time they fell in love and were married three years later. The groom will soon be thirty-one, the bride a couple of years younger. They knew what they wanted and know how very blessed they are to have found each other. And guess what?

Our family feels blessed too!

P.S. Almost three years later and our couple is doing great! Thank you God!

Chapter 4 Fun With My Aunts

My mother was a collector; "a holder-on of interesting stuff," almost a hoarder type of woman. Unfortunately I am more like her than I ever wanted to be. My sister found an interesting letter that my mother wrote in 1938. It was written to my Aunt Emily, Aunt Helen, my brother and myself. I was three and a half years old, my brother almost two. My dad had been asked to present a paper at a professional conference in California.

This happened in 1939, long before airlines were an option. Long- distance calls were very expensive so unless there was a death in the family or something equally important, long-distance calls were not made. People wrote real "snail mail" letters, or sent telegrams, which were expensive but not as costly as phone calls.

My parents, along with my dad's parents, drove to California. (They could have taken the train for this big adventure; however, they drove. Probably this was the only time my grandparents ever got out of Ohio.) They all wanted to stop to see the sights along the way. I believe the trip took three to four weeks.

They left my brother and me in the care of my mother's younger sisters, Aunt Emily, who was about twenty-three, and Aunt Helen, who was thirteen or fourteen. It is hard for me to believe that they would go off and leave a three-and-a-half-year-old and an almost two-year-old.

When they returned my brother didn't remember them, which crushed my mother. (He was always – according to my sister – Mother's favorite.) I thought my sister was the favorite.

I just know I wasn't.

I remember taking walks with my aunts during this time. My brother was pushed in his carriage. I remember the "chocolate milk incident" like it happened yesterday. I had always been allowed to have chocolate milk – not a wise habit to start – in my opinion. I remember sitting at the kitchen table; Aunt Emily was sitting to my left, Aunt Helen to my right and my brother across from me in a high chair. One day at lunch, there in front of me was white milk. I asked Aunt Emily where my chocolate milk was. I remember her saying very sarcastically, "The chocolate cow died."

A few days later after not drinking the white milk, I had chocolate milk again. Being a smart-ass three-and-one-half-year-old, I asked her how I got chocolate milk since the chocolate cow died. She, very sharply, told me the dairy got a new chocolate cow. I have to say she was pissed at me. (This was when the milkman would deliver milk from the dairy to the front door.)

This is a letter written by my mother to my aunts, brother and me:

Dear Emily, Helen, Emily Jo & Larry,

Arrived here a short time ago in Rapid City, South Dakota. It's at the foot of the Black Hills with Mt. Rushmore where the presidents' faces are carved out of the granite mountain.

We are staying in a Professor's (of the school here) home. This afternoon we saw the Bad Lands. They were really terrible looking and it was a strange sight. We drove for miles and miles never seeing a tree.

I presume our last letter arrived early Tuesday morning. That was the best we could do in that town. We traveled 1361 miles since we left home Sunday.

The eats have been good all the way and very reasonable. We have lots to see tomorrow so must get to bed. Hoping that our darlings are O.K. Give them each a big kiss and hug for us.

> *We will send another telegram from Yellowstone Nat. Park.*

From time to time you will hear from us, in some form.

With Love & Kisses

Rose & Lee

My dad had one sibling who was married to our Aunt Bobbie. I thought she was a cool aunt. She always remembered our birthdays with sweet little gifts like coloring books and crayons when we were in grade school, birthday cards and notes as we got older. After we moved about thirty-five miles away from Martinsville, when I was fourteen, we saw Daddy's relatives less often.

All of my aunts were unique in their own way but my Aunt Emily was "something else." She would set her alarm to get up early on Monday mornings to get her sheets and clothes on the clothesline before any of her neighbors. She worked with Aunt Helen during World War II in Akron, Ohio, as a riveter on airplanes. When the war was over she married Uncle Karl. They had one daughter, Ada Marie, who was named after my grandmother, also Aunt Emily's mother. Aunt Emily molded Ada Marie, in my mind, into the most perfect person I have ever known. Get this, my aunt had her daughter put on gloves before putting on her pantyhose. Can you imagine? Ada Marie was a straight-A student but after college rebelled by marrying the love of her life, who was a Catholic. FYI, they met in college and he was a terrific guy. They had three young children when she died at thirty-five of cancer.

My aunt went through a lot. She was there when her dad, then her mom died, as well as her husband, who died of a heart attack while shoveling snow. Then having to see her daughter fight and lose her battle with cancer.

Aunt Helen lived with us during World War II while Uncle Paul was in Japan. As the years passed they would often come to see us. They were really a fun couple, always teasing each other and us.

They lived about thirty-five miles from Mary Washington College. Uncle Paul would frequently come get me so I could spend the weekend or holidays with them. I was blessed in that all my aunts worked and were strong women in an age when most women did not work. Aunt Emily worked as a bookkeeper, when Ada Marie was in high school and college. Aunt Helen became an assistant at the library and wrote a book about her life, which my sister edited and published for the family. Aunt Bobbie taught elementary school. They were all very loving to me.

I still miss them.

Chapter 5 *Fun With Balls*

I love to shoot hoops. I used to love to play softball, croquet and to bowl. What kind of balls did you expect me to talk about? Oh – those. Well, girlie, aren't you glad you don't have to deal with "those"? Maybe that's why guys aren't as smart as we are. They are using their brain cells managing their equipment instead of THINKING. Am I right? I really feel sorry for them as they are so clueless about us gals, even though some of the older guys "think" they understand us. Most never will!

How many of you watch the pros? Frankly, I prefer college basketball. I love, love, love "March Madness." Most of you that haven't watched the play-offs – try it sometime. Really fun especially if your college makes it to the finals. Lots of people love to watch baseball. I prefer the pros; however, I like playing softball or basketball more than watching it on television. My favorite team has always been "The Yankees" but we did live in the Atlanta area for almost forty years. So – "Go Braves, Go!"

Did you ever see the movie "Jerry Maguire"? Lots of gals I know had real crushes on Tom Cruise. Why, I don't really understand. Okay, he was cute but I guess I never lusted after short guys. He didn't turn out to be the best of marriage material, did he? Speaking of short guys, how about Johnny Depp? Cute too, but obviously not good at making lasting marriages either.

I feel so sorry for each and every child of divorce. My biggest hope for mankind is for people, all people, to live in peace and love. Couples should be more careful of who and when they choose their partners and parenthood. They need to love each other and care enough for their children to stay together. That means getting past lust to find out what kind of a person they are falling in love with – really. That way you won't end up with a jerk who makes you pregnant to keep you. (Putting holes in the condoms.) Yes, I know of a guy who did that. Speaking of balls, I met a businesswoman who told me that after making a business speech a co-worker said, in an unkind way, "You certainly have balls, lady!" The next day she called some veterinarians and found some Great Dane testicles. She took them home, cut them up and fried them; put them into a to-go box. GROSS, yes. She delivered them to the guy's office. She said, "Now you have balls too!" Isn't that a GREAT story? I heard this story many years ago from the gal who did this. I couldn't make this up, cookie.

My friend Vivian played tennis until almost ninety, as did one of my neighbors. Another friend's husband, a long-time player, saves tennis balls for my Dal. Both he and Viv had both knees replaced. Tennis does keep you exercising and chasing balls too. P.S. Are you a ball-chaser??? I'm just asking.

P.P.S. I guess the orthopedic doctors love tennis players and probably get to take lots of vacations because of them.

Chapter 6 *Fun At Funerals*

You liked the chapter by this name in *Hold on to Your Panties and Have Fun*, so I decided to tell you about my recent funeral transgressions. Yes, I am bad and, yes, sometimes I do get disgusted with myself.

Thank God Mama isn't around to see me.

Those of you who don't know me are asking, "What bad stuff can she do at funerals?" Well, I introduce myself to people I haven't met and, yes, I sometimes do give them one of my bookmarks. "That is not so bad," you say. Well, I don't think so either, but you can see that maybe a funeral is not an appropriate time for self-promotion. A bit tasteless maybe or a lot tasteless depending upon your degree of judgmentalness. I remember that I might have given my first book to a widow at her husband's funeral. Hey, isn't it the time for her to lighten up and get on with her life? How about getting an attractive older widow to laugh at graveside? How? I just told her she was the sexiest widow I had ever seen. Hey, it just slipped out. Her husband would have loved it.

A close friend lost her husband. (He was buried with a military funeral in a cemetery in Florida.) Since I could not go, she sent me a photo of her with the casket. How sweet, but I wasn't sweet. I said, "I am really shocked at what you wore." She said, "Why, was my dress too short?" "No, but I couldn't believe you wore Bar-Hopping Shoes." Thankfully, she took it as something to laugh about. This friend, who I adore, is a very good Baptist. But you know I'll do almost anything for a laugh.

Try as hard as I can, I'll never be "a lady" like my mother hoped and prayed for. No way. No wonder she died young at eighty-eight. I just hope my skin stays as good as hers.

When one of my best friends died in 2013, the minister asked if anyone wanted to say something about her. Surprise, surprise, surprise, I was the first. When I first met Cheryl she was running around the dog show ring in little black combat shoes and black socks. (Hey, at least they matched.) She wore a long flowing skirt. (They laughed, as pantyhose, good looking flats and attractive straight, or A-line, tailored outfits are the norm.) Another friend had asked me to "clue Cheryl in to appropriate attire." Tactless Emily told her, "Cheryl, if you want to win you need to get rid of the ugly socks and combat boots. You need to dress like a professional and wear pantyhose and flats." Well, the poor thing cried. (I heard later.) I was asked to apologize. Not a problem as I have to do THAT a lot! I told her my intent was NOT to hurt her feelings but to help her. We ended up co-owning and breeding champions that Cheryl showed. She learned to appreciate my candor and my always "telling it like it is." At the memorial picnic I asked her husband, Buddy, "Did Cheryl tell you about what I said to her about getting a young lover?" He grinned.

"No, what was it?" I told him, "I said, 'Cheryl, you know how I am always telling you to NOT do anything I wouldn't? Well, now I am telling you at this point in your life...' (She had been turned over to Hospice.) '...to do whatever you damn well please. Furthermore, I think this is the perfect time to take a young lover.' Normally it would get a big belly laugh, but I got a tiny giggle. Then I said, 'Can you picture y'all having sex in your recliner with your oxygen tank?' Another small laugh." Her hubby laughed when I told him!

Cheryl and I shared our love of people, fun and Dalmatians, dog shows and certain TV shows such as "Dancing with the Stars," "American Idol," "The Voice" and "Monk." She was a very loving sister-friend to me. She always answered the phone with a cheery "Hello." She was fun and loved to "get me" with her humor, as I did her. And get this. Cheryl was the perfect customer for Hallmark. She sent her friends and relatives cards for every occasion. She also gave me several of the "Maxine" books. I finally asked her, "Cheryl, am I crabby as the Maxine character?" "No," she said, "but you do have an edge and are so good at verbal comebacks." That's good enough for me. I will say, she did drive me a bit crazy with her every-holiday Hallmark cards. Finally I sent her an index card. I wrote, "Happy New Year, Happy Valentine's Day, Happy Birthday, Happy St. Paddy's Day, Happy Easter, Happy Memorial Day, Happy Fourth of July, Happy Labor Day, Happy Thanksgiving, Merry Christmas and Happy any holiday I missed." A couple of years ago she had brought the index card to a dog show to show our friends and me. We all had a big laugh. I miss that gal and yes, I'll miss getting her fun cards.

Funerals are not fun but sometimes "funny stuff" happens at funerals.

P.S. Have you written your obituary yet? I did mine – just in case I go soon. I want to always have the last word, don't you?

🍷

Fun With My Best Friend Joan Rivers

Many of us were sad when our friend Joan Rivers died. I remember her from her first Johnny Carson performance. She was funny when doing family type humor. As time went on she got more edgy and yes, downright, some would say, raunchy. The mark of a "true comic" is getting people to laugh at clean humor. Believe me, raunchy is much easier.

What many may not know is how hard she worked. According to Donald Trump, her work ethic and energy surpassed most all of the people he had on his television show "The Apprentice." She apparently was like an "Energizer bunny." Could Joan have been wearing vibrating panties? It's a joke, okay? Nothing would surprise me – about my "best friend," Joan. If you believe she was my "bestie," I have a lot of swamp land in Florida I could sell you.

The days after her unexpected death I watched a lot of television footage about Joan. The one thing I can't understand is why she kept having more and more plastic surgery. Okay, I get it, she was not a beauty, and few of us are. Money was never a problem so yes, I would have had my nose done had I been her. Later, I might have had a mini-lift, which is lifting anything south of the nose. I really would like to do that.

(However, I am chicken, chicken, chicken so I probably won't.) Would you?

FYI: I checked and it does cost a couple of thousand for a mini-lift and about four or five thousand for a full face/neck lift.

P.S. I hear there are some new procedures with lasers to avoid cutting and stitching.

What I found very admirable about Joan is that she was such a giving person. Her daughter, Melissa, produced a special for PBS about Joan, and I learned a lot more information about her. Every year early on Thanksgiving Day, she would take her adorable grandson, Cooper, on a trip around New York taking food that her cook had made to those less fortunate and shut-ins. She had been doing this for years.

Another surprising fact I learned was how elaborate and how large her New York apartment was. She joked that it was the apartment Anne Boleyn would have had if she had been rich. In her living room there was lots and lots of applied wood trim, high ceilings over the elaborate drapery treatments, plus beautiful French antique furniture. Her bedroom looked even more over the top with more antiques and lots of draping surrounding her bed. I expected her to have lovely surroundings but I imagined a more traditional or a dashing contemporary look. Maybe she had a secret desire to be royal. What do you think? Her father was a doctor in the day they could make big bucks, so maybe a lot of furniture was inherited. Wonder what dear Melissa will do with all that stuff? Did you see Joan's closet on "Fashion Police"? It was full of beautiful clothes.

Hey, boys, (meaning my sons) you might have been more embarrassed if Joan had been your mom. Often I have felt sorry for Melissa. If you have Comcast maybe you could pull up Joan Knows Best, or whatever their reality show was called. (Now I know Melissa is playing her mom in a not-yet-out movie for television or theater, I don't know.)

Poor Melissa sure was embarrassed when her mom invaded her privacy in the shower, as well as during sex. Can you imagine, sons, if I had done that to you? Still, I'm sure Melissa misses her mom.

P.S. Speaking of celebrities I wonder what Jimmy Buffett would do had I been his mom??? Hey, if I had been famous, he probably would have written a song about me. Or, possibly I could have made me a "bad-ass momma" in one of his books. What do you think? If you haven't heard his music or read his books you have missed out. Time to get with it, baby. FYI, Jimmy's books take place in Florida or Cuba and are very interesting.

Fun With Jay Leno

Do I know him? Not yet, but I bet we would really have a great time (at least I would.) Hey, we have a lot in common as we both love, love, love cars and we are both fun and funny people.

I've been a fan of Jay since he first appeared with Johnny Carson on "The Tonight Show." Then I loved him as host of "The Tonight Show." Now, I love his new show, "Jay Leno's Garage."

You know I like learning new stuff. While watching Jay's show on fifties sports cars I learned that out of the 1956 Corvette, the 1955 Thunderbird (one of the first cars to have seat belts) and the 1958 British MG, the one that an expert said was the best investment was – DRUM ROLL please – the Corvette! Currently, it is worth eighty-two thousand dollars. The Thunderbird comes in second at fifty thousand dollars, and the 1958 MG is last at thirty-five thousand dollars. The Corvette is loved not only for its lines but for its speed. The Thunderbird is also said to be powerful but doesn't have quite the number of fans as the Corvette. The British MG 1958 was valued for its "neat look" and because you have fun zipping around curves with the wind in your hair.

I didn't realize that the first cars were powered by steam. In 1803 the Stanley Steamer gained a lot of fans. It was fast at 127 miles per hour. Or maybe that was the Double Steam Car. Probably built by Stanley Steamer, I'm not real sure.

Every year I try to go to the Amelia Concours d' Elegance held on Amelia Island. It is quite "the thing" to go to, if you like cars. They have a parade that is free – all other events require pricey entrance fees. Hubby and I go to look at the cars the day before the big show is completely set up. It is interesting. What is especially nice is there are a lot less people. They have several big auctions like the ones seen on the car channel, which require paid admission. We went once before they started charging. It's very, very, very interesting to see people bidding thousands and thousands and sometimes even millions of dollars for these collectable autos. All the ticket money, after expenses, goes to a worthy cause. I would guess some people take it off their taxes. Who knows? If you are super-wealthy and enter your car in the show or auction "I hear" you are invited to some fun dinner parties held at the Ritz or the Amelia Island Plantation (now owned by the Omni).
Doesn't this sound like fun?

Wondering if Jay goes to the one held at Pebble Beach, California? I'm betting he does.

P.S. Jay, come to Florida and we could hang out. Hey, Jay, I love "car guys." I know I could learn a lot about cars from you, baby. And we would have fun cracking each other up as I love Comedians too!

Fun With Rob Lowe

No, I haven't met him but I feel I know him from his television appearances, especially on "Who Do You Think You Are?" I know he is from my home state – Ohio. I think he is from Lima.

He looks better with make-up, don't you think? I do feel someone ought to have bought this guy a really good razor. Apparently his beard grows out very fast. Can he have a beard problem or maybe a poor razor or maybe he is just lazy or going for the Don Johnson look? This show was shot in Washington, D.C., Trenton, New Jersey and in several German locations. Maybe Rob and Don Johnson or Tom Cruise could do a remake of "Grumpy Old Men" since they are not exactly the "pretty boys" they used to be. What do you think?

P.S. I hear he is on the comeback trail in 2018 with maybe a facelift and for sure a shave in the promo I saw briefly. This promo was for, I believe, a television show or movie.

P.P.S. He looked damn good. Who was your doctor, Rob?

Chapter 8 Fun With Bimbos and Jerks

Actually, I haven't had that much experience with bimbos. However, I had an experience with a gal I really think is a bimbo – and she isn't a blonde. I'll let you decide if you think she is a bimbo.

This is what happened at the drive-thru bank window. I wanted to cash a check for two hundred dollars. I wanted one hundred dollars in twenties, seventy in tens and thirty dollars in fives. I probably should have written all this out. This really confused the young gal. I had to go over it several times. Gee whiz, couldn't she write it down?? It took forever – I counted my cash and I did get my two hundred dollars but not in the amounts I had asked for. This took close to a half an hour so I gave up and drove away. Seems like she was a bimbo.

Question: Don't little kids play store with toy money anymore? Next time I went to that bank I didn't see her so maybe they figured out she was in the wrong job or really is a bimbo. Thank God most bimbos see me coming and seem to get out of my way.

I think of bimbos as gals – jerks, definitely guys. I seem to run into a few of them from time to time. I think jerks are primarily twenty-something- year-old guys who just haven't gotten it together, but they think they have. While most jerks grow up, bimbos never change – unfortunately. Another name for these people could be clueless. Kind of like those that are walking down the street looking at their phones nearly falling into a man-hole or running into an old bitch like me. They better not do that – or watch out. Don't make the old bitch mad, is all I'm saying. I pray a lot when I'm driving, as almost every day I hear of some innocent person or persons being killed by a bimbo or ultra-jerk on their cell. Pay attention! Your life could depend on it!

P.S. I just heard on television that every year during the summer months, new teenage drivers kill thousands of people with their careless driving.

P.P.S. I recently heard of a fifty-year-old guy who was driving his mom and dad's car with his ten-year-old son – at eighty miles per hour while texting. What were you thinking, jerk?

Chapter 9 *Fun With Polka-Dot Puppies and Dogs*

"If dogs don't go to heaven, I want to go where they go." Do you know who said that? You're so young you wouldn't know. I remember him. First hint – a guy as an old man, in the black-and-white news reels. Second hint, before movies were in color. Third hint, he was an internationally well-known person. Fourth hint, he often hung out with famous people. Fifth and last hint, he was a humorist. Who is he? Think about it, or look it up, baby. I love the quote in that he wants to go where dogs go. I do too! As much as I love people, I may love dogs even more. They are just easier than most people, aren't they?

Wondering if my dog is smarter than I am? My dog knows when it is time to "call it a day." I guess I don't, as frequently the clock gets to midnight before I make my move. Diva, the Dalmatian, is ready to go to bed by eleven. She looks at me, gets up and stands in front of me and then looks at the door. Slowly she moves towards it. I let her out, she tinkles, comes back in and heads for her bed in the laundry room. She wants her biscuits, now!

My Hubby tells me she figures out when I am almost done with a phone call. She'll be lying on the entry hall rug near the living room where Hubby is reading. When she thinks I am almost done, she gets up and moves towards me as I finish chatting with a friend. How does she know? I haven't figured it out. Maybe this is why I should have STUPID engraved on my forehead?

When Diva knows it is time to be fed, around five, she comes to me and just looks at me, wagging her tail. If I am sitting down she will put her head on the arm of my chair or on my knee and look up at me as adorably as she can, of course wagging her entire body. Most of my past dogs would bark – not her – she just continues with her charming pleading. According to our youngest son, she has more toys than he and his brother had growing up. Hey, son, if you had been like Diva you might have gotten more. Cheryl and Buddy deserve credit for Diva's good behavior.

She was a beautiful beast when I handed her over to them at eight weeks. Diva is bright, most Dals are, but she is much more obedient than most I have had. Or perhaps she is less willful than some. She learned very quickly, after one verbal correction, not to go in our bedrooms and not to jump on the furniture or us.

Someone asked me if I showed in obedience. I said, "Hell, no, I'm not obedience trained." All I ever required of our Dals was that they come when called, stay off the furniture and us, to hush, to stay out of the bedrooms, walk on a lead, and not "go potty" in their crate or the house. Diva is asked to jump into her crate in my van. This Buddy taught her at eight years while visiting us. I just couldn't pick her up anymore due to my hip and back issues.

Buddy and Cheryl had Diva for only a year before Clover, another of our girls, jumped her. It was their fault for not being extra careful when the bitches were "in season." Bitches can sometimes be temperamental. In this case they had taken Diva to the Dalmatian Club of America Specialty Show and had been gone a week. They brought Diva in the house and Clover was jealous of Diva getting to go and not her; thus a fight began. Had Cheryl exercised Diva in the front yard while

Buddy took Clover out to the back yard, then put Diva in a crate instead of putting them together and basically ignoring Diva for a few days, I really believe the dogs would not have gotten into it.

In this case we were the lucky ones as we got Diva about six weeks before our Dal, Tex, died. I might have been Dal-less if Diva had not come at that time.

I love, love, love puppies! On a recent trip to Norfolk, Virginia, I got to play with thirteen beautiful, happy, tail wagging adorable little spotted eight-week-old clowns. What fun! What a litter. One of the loveliest Dal litters I have ever seen. They had beautiful, sweet, open spotting with a few freckled spotting around their noses. Their spotting ranged from nice, lightly marked, to medium in spotting. None were heavily marked, no ugly "whities," and none that are going to be too heavy in markings. Their eyes were rimmed like eyeliner, their nose leathers completely covered, except for two boys who just had a small amount of pigment yet to cover. We did get five blue eyes, which is acceptable in the show ring but not something I would want to breed. The reason is that while double blue eyes are very striking, one blue and one dark brown I don't believe are as attractive. Many breeders have experienced a connection between blue eyes and deafness. Fortunately, in almost fifty years of breeding I seldom have had a deaf puppy. However, forty years ago with an outcross I had a large litter of eleven with only two blue/brown-eyed "eachies"; both turned out to be deaf. This litter was hearing tested as are all of our puppies. We had only one uni, meaning the puppy could hear in one ear but not the other. She had one blue eye. (She was sold as a pet – not to be bred.) She will be spayed before she is a year of age. We had no patches, who have big black areas present at birth and should never be bred.

All of my co-breeders do a lot of testing. Like their parents, all the puppies are hearing tested at about five weeks. The litters later will have hip testing as well as thyroid (not usually a Dal problem) and eye testing. Most of our litters are bilateral – meaning all can hear in both ears. We breed for happy healthy dogs. If we line breed (meaning breeding dogs who have common relatives maybe three generations back) we get lovely personalities and healthy, very happy, outgoing sweet babies.

The Norfolk litter is exceptional in that on the sire's side they go back to a back-cross-Pointer. Years ago scientists started breeding the Pointer into their bloodlines to eliminate kidney issues that could cause Dalmatians (usually males) to block up, meaning small crystals of calcium would interfere with their urination and cause pain. If surgery isn't done in time the poor animal will die. This litter was DNA tested through the University of California at Davis, California, and it was found the only one who tested positive in normal Dalmatian function was the uni. All the rest are non-carriers of the gene that causes blockage. If these Dals are bred they will help the breed.

Any testing is expensive but, believe me, testing is important in making our breed even better. Over three days I spent fourteen to fifteen hours with these puppies and know they are exceptional. Time will tell what they will contribute. Most will not get into show/breeding homes but will be super-attractive fun pets.

I would like to see temperament testing done on every adult dog before he or she gets their championship. Some lines have what I consider bad temperament. When a show dog growls at a person or another dog or tries to bite someone, they should NEVER be bred.

P.S. I love puppy kisses and watching spotted puppies playing. Dals require obedience training as they are like a bright four-year-old. Meaning they can get into mischief very quickly. They are not for the faint of heart, girlfriend. They will take over if you are not head bitch at your house. They are cute, sweet, loyal and good alarm dogs. (Meaning they bark when the doorbell rings but are not normally barkers.) They are easy to groom, not picky eaters and are not yappy dogs. When trained correctly, they are absolute joys with bright clown-like personalities. They remember people they met years before and will act like your friend is their returning owner.

I guess that is why my friends like Diva so much.

P.S. The guy who said he wanted to go where the dogs go was Mark Twain.

Chapter 10 *Fun Saying Yes to the Dress*

Okay, so I am somewhat addicted to Bravo's "Say Yes to the Dress." I'm wondering how much of this reality show is scripted. What do you think?

I find some of these girls' budgets unbelievable. One girl spent one hundred thousand dollars on her dress. Can you believe that? I can't. It was beautiful with a lot of French custom lace with hand-stitched crystals. The veil was super lovely! Kinda scalloped edging with attached crystals.

The bride's wedding gown plus the bride's mother's dress and the six bridesmaids' dresses totaled six hundred thousand dollars. They were from South Africa, black and beautiful. Wonder how Daddy made his money???

Another bride with an unlimited budget ended up with a designer gown which combined three dresses. It priced out at forty-five thousand dollars. Are these girls crazy? Think about putting most of that towards a home or to feed the homeless. What amazes me the most is the people who come to help "pick out" the dress. Why? I'm not sure. The father comes to give his opinion, the mother (who is sometimes "the bitch mamma"), an aunt or two and any number of bridesmaids. If the bride is lucky she'll have only three or four people giving her grief. I can see taking an honest friend or your mom with you. Since I paid for my dress myself I did it all on my own. A recent plus-sized bride came in with her mom and a couple of other women. The entire family had gone on vacation two weeks earlier. The whole family was in shock as the bride's dad dropped dead of a heart attack while they were on that "special vacation." The wedding was coming up soon and it was very difficult for her. The store didn't have too many options for this plus-size gal. White fluffy gowns don't make one look slim. Fortunately the bridal consultant found one that apparently had good support on top, with a draped waist that held her in and made her look slimmer. It was so sad to think of her dad not being able to walk her down the aisle.

I've noticed that most brides are buying strapless dresses. Some have very full skirts with a lot of tulle and or lace. Some of the gals are going for mermaid dresses that flare out above or below the knee. Very few are opting for dresses that have really long trains. My granddaughter was able to unsnap her train after the wedding for dancing. What a clever idea. Some brides decide to have a dress to wear at the wedding, plus another wedding gown for their party afterwards. This, I feel, is unnecessary. But, girlfriend, what do I know?

Frankly, spending big bucks on a wedding is not necessary. Isn't it better to have a simpler wedding without credit card debt? Couldn't the money be better spent going towards the down payment on a condo or house, or paying off college loans? The wedding and party are over before you know it.

Am I being too practical? Maybe. What do you think?

Remember the huge wedding I talked about in my first book? It was like a big movie production. A friend of mine talked me into "crashing." I can only guess what the country club party cost for a church full of people. No, Joan and I didn't crash that, but I'm willing to bet Daddy could spend one hundred thousand dollars today on a wedding like that. Another bride I know spent a lot less and had what I heard was a beautiful small church wedding with a country reception. Her awesome dress cost her around four hundred and fifty-five dollars. She is a very clever gal who used flowers from her parents' yard along with local flowers for her bouquet, bridesmaids and the reception. The wedding was held in the back yard of her parents' country home. The bride bought hanging strings of lights to hang around the dance floor. I believe she had friends who provided the music. It sounded so sweet – just like the bride.

If you're thinking of getting married – don't rush it. Slow and easy going, please. Challenge yourself to pay as you go, without credit card debt, like my sweet mountain friend did.

Chapter 11 *Fun With Sarah*

I met Sarah when she was in her early forties while I interviewed her for a market research firm. We found out that we were both members of the Atlanta Kennel Club. She was happily married. Her English husband was employed as an engineer for Lockheed. Sarah and her husband had just returned to Atlanta from the Middle East, where her husband had worked for several years. They took some of the money they made and bought some beautiful rugs before coming home. They purchased a lovely brick ranch in a prestigious area of Atlanta with five acres. At the same time Sarah opened a dog grooming shop in an upscale shopping center. They went to dog shows showing their "Serwen Yorkies." A woman who seemed to be Sarah's best friend told Sarah's husband that Sarah was having an affair. The trouble-maker described a car that was at their house several times a week; Sarah's husband drove past and saw that this was true. However, he did not investigate. (It was a girlfriend's car.) Then "Trouble" came onto Sarah's husband. Sarah came home early one evening to find him on top of "Trouble." Sarah went berserk! She clawed at his back. That was it! They were divorced! All Sarah got was "the dogs," the grooming shop, the household goods, furniture and enough money for a very small house.

Her lovely life changed drastically. She worked hard and she saved her money. I lost touch for a while. Then I heard she was "in love." I advised her to go slowly. Next thing I knew, he had talked her into opening a beautiful mattress store. I, for "some reason," didn't trust him. She had several "break-ins" with lots of the most expensive mattresses taken. Police finally caught the thief and it was her partner in business as well as in bed. Sarah was heartbroken and broke again. She went from driving a "new Caddie" while married to her first husband, to twenty years later driving a van that had over two hundred thousand miles – looked horrible but ran. We lost touch again. One day she called me and I asked if I could call her back. She said, "No, I can't talk long." She went on to tell me she was in Grady Hospital (where people with no money go). She had cancer and she was to have surgery the next day. I told her I would call her son later to see how she was doing. He was now running the grooming shop. Sarah and her son had moved in together.

The next day I found out I had to have surgery soon. I became obsessed with cleaning and house projects. It turned out I had ovarian cancer. I was very lucky with mine as it was just a grade one; whereas Sarah went through treatment, I did not. We kept in touch by phone.

About six weeks after I got out of the hospital I took Sarah out to lunch. We went to a historic restaurant across from the governor's mansion. She looked nice. She had lost weight, had make-up on and a pretty wig. We went to an art exhibit as we both loved art. I took her home and we hung out until she told me she had to have a nap. That, sadly was the last time I saw her. She died shortly afterwards.

I learned a lot from her about spirituality. I began going to the Unity Church because of her. I cautiously learned to trust people. I learned to love people even when they had been "shitty" to me. I have learned that Yorkies have very little bladders and – unless just bathed – smell more than larger dogs. I learned to try to make the best of every day because you don't know when you'll be leaving. I learned that wigs look a hell of a lot better than bald heads.

Whenever I think of Sarah, I feel sad as I still miss her, thirty years later. I also miss my college roommates, Mary Lou and Barb, really good neighbor, Ginny, my dear co-Dalbreeder friend, Cheryl, and dear, sweet Melody. For your information, this is why I keep myself out there to meet younger people as I hope you will do.

P.S. I know my friends would have loved my books.

Chapter 12 **Fun Missing a Plane Again**

On a trip to Norfolk, Virginia, in the fall of 2015 I missed a connecting flight that began in Jacksonville, Florida. I could have gone out of Charlotte, North Carolina, Atlanta or Jacksonville. I had my Hubby look up the prices. They were all about the same. Interestingly, there was less than ten dollars difference. I believe the ONLY direct flight was from Charlotte. It was early A.M. and I am NOT an early bird as my favorite readers will tell you. I also would have to deal with boarding my Dalmatian, Diva. I chose not to drive, as not only is it a twelve-hour drive, but I had a van full of important stuff like banker boxes of research and writing to complete, plus items I wanted to take back to Florida from North Carolina. As we would probably be selling our wonderful mountain home next year, I had household items, boxes of book stuff, Diva's extra-large crate, her folding hotel crate, dog food, two large coolers, two suitcases plus clothes on hangers. All of this secured with bungee cords as I always leave plenty of visual room. I decided to go home to Florida, then to fly out of Jacksonville.

Hubby stayed longer in North Carolina to shampoo the carpet, tidy the yard and to have ten days of quiet away from the two bitches (Diva and me.) I chose to take a taxi service to the airport. It wasn't cheap but it saved me time finding a parking space, parking the car, extra walking, etc. I know I could have gotten a neighbor or friend to take me but I hate to ask others to do stuff for me. My driver was right on time. Miracle of miracles, so was I.

I had just gotten home two days before I was to fly out. It usually takes me a week to pack or unpack my van. I had an appointment with my chiropractor, Dr. Hottie, and an appointment with my nail gal and a trip to Walgreen's, etc., that I needed to do before I left. It was a hectic, hectic, hectic time. Top all of this off with not getting enough sleep for a week, as well as the beginning of a cold.

Fortunately, everything began well! I found out something that you may want to know when flying. ALL airlines overbook so if you want an assigned seat you need to get to the gate and the airline agent early. Otherwise, you may not get on. I wasn't feeling super so wasn't as alert as I should have been. Unfortunately, when I looked at my connecting flight information I saw three twenty-six P.M. and thought that was the time my connecting flight in Washington, D.C.'s Dulles airport left. I had a salad for lunch and enjoyed talking with an eleven-year-old girl and her dad from Indiana, AND – missed my flight out of Dulles. I was supposed to get into Norfolk at three twenty-six instead of leaving. I had to wait a couple of hours.

For lunch I had a mimosa. (I love mimosas because the orange juice perks me up while the vodka relaxes me. Truly one is enough and that is all I had.) I was super-tired and when I looked at my schedule, I thought I was flying out several hours later. I had gone to my gate – plenty early, I thought – only to find out my flight left thirty minutes before. So, instead of getting to Norfolk at around four it would be after six P.M. Ugh – that is IF I could get on the flight. I was basically on stand-by. A sweet young guy asked me if I knew anything about the voucher program. I told him I thought that you get three hundred dollars off an American flight and it was transferable. He took the voucher program deal and I got on in the last two minutes – literally. NOT fun, I can tell you. But I met some interesting people and had a lot of fun and handed out lots of bookmarks. I also met a couple of interesting seatmates. One a sweet handsome gay black guy. (My youngest is gay, so I can relate.) He was a business health care administrator who had a master's degree in the field. When he learned nurses made a lot more money than he was making he went back to school and became a nurse. This man also travels and gives talks at hospitals about managing health care. A smart, smart, smart and fun, fun, fun guy! My friend met me at the airport minutes after I called her. I checked in at a nice motel near her house. There was no room at my friend's house for this old bitch as she lives with her three adult kids. Not a problem as I want peace and quiet, my air filter and my own seventy-four-degree room with a firm mattress and super-clean bedding, please. What is worse than being a "pain in the ass" is KNOWING you are one. My friend and I proceeded to her house. Her middle kid had fixed dinner and wanted to know how I wanted my steak. While I was there her daughter drove me to the motel and twice to dinner, as well as helping her mom and I try to sort out puppies. (There were four girls and nine boys.) Her oldest son gave me a harp concert. Cool kids, sweet, helpful, respectful and fun!

The puppy sorting was a nightmare. I have NEVER seen so many puppies who looked so much alike! Beautiful heads, lovely bodies and none too white or missing trim on eye rims or nose trim. No heavy, too- dark spotting, none too light. They were healthy, happy tail-wagging, get into-mischief, fun kissy-face puppies. Being in Dalmatians almost fifty years and having had some lovely litters, this one is overall one of the best litters I have seen! All the beautiful little faces looked so similar!

We started sorting with the girls. First we had one uni, meaning she could hear in only one ear; she could have been shown as she had lovely, medium spotting, but we had a spay/neuter home for a beautiful pet. Then we had three show girls. After watching them move – a lot – we selected one to keep to show and later hopefully breed. One of the girls is going to a friend who has a lovely male out of my breeding that she is showing. It only took us a couple of hours to sort the girls.

The boys, the boys, the boys – nine! We looked at each boy several times. From mid-morning to dinner time. Then another couple of hours to be followed by four to five hours the next day before I left. They were so adorable and so lovely it was very hard to pick out three for the show homes we had. There were at least four or five more that could have probably finished their championships. WOW. I wish I could see them all as adults.

By the time this book comes out, I will have owned, shown and bred Atlantis Dalmatians for over fifty years. Thanks to several co-owners who have let me help them with the genetics, I have been able to keep my bloodlines going even though I haven't had a litter myself in over twenty-five years. Can't wait to see our babies winning in the ring!

P.S. I made it home with no problems – just fun with seatmates and stewards and of course the pilots. I always tell them I will be rating their landings and they always laugh. They laugh again when I give them a B, B+ or C. Well, not many C's. Those pilots always explain why it wasn't the greatest. I just smile and wave.   Flying can be fun if you want it to be.

Chapter 13 Fun With The Neighbors

At present, we have homes in Florida and North Carolina, both in small towns located in small neighborhoods. I love our neighbors but some of them are a bit strange. You might call them – "overinvolved." It seems that some neighbors seem to need to know everything going on in the entire neighborhood. Maybe they need to get a life. Some of them spend a great deal of money updating their homes. Maybe that gives these people a right to be nosy, or does it? Okay, I can see keeping our homes, property and neighborhood safe and attractive to keep the values up. However, even though I like people, I am not overly close to my neighbors. I love seeing them at neighborhood parties and at community events. I am not one to pop over unannounced, nor do I want someone knocking on my door, catching me in the middle of a project or in my p.j.s writing.

I grew up in the country and value my privacy. I try to be a good neighbor by taking a plate of brownies to new neighbors. I wave as I drive by and often stop to chat a minute, but I don't get too involved. We have busy lives and don't want to get too close.

Good neighbors look out for one another. For example, two different neighbors have called us about problems at our Florida house when we were out of town. Guess what? They received Omaha Steaks for being so nice. I try to be sweet and nice; however, as my fans know, this isn't easy for me.

I would love to have a party but that requires tidying and cleaning. That is difficult if you are busy, busy, busy! Maybe someday, after I get this and another book done, maybe.

While reading an article on keeping your neighborhood safe, I learned that it is very important to keep our lawn clean and mowed. We also need to keep our home entrance visible. Our neighbors do this, thank God. It is good to know your neighbors. (I know the close ones.) It was also suggested that we join a website such as www.nextdoor.com. This is said to be a secure network. It is designed for neighbors who want to post events or ask questions. Another suggestion is to "friend" your local law enforcement. This is possible in many communities. Be aware of what goes on in your neighborhood, be friendly and alert officials of unusual events. This is very important! If you see or hear unusual things happening at night on a regular basis, you need to let your law enforcement know. In 2015, a neighbor of the mass murderer in San Bernardino, California, said she noticed a lot of nighttime activity and wished she had reported it.

Most importantly, enjoy your home and your neighborhood. Value your home by keeping it up. That means power washing your driveway and the exterior of your house and painting it when it needs to be painted. This means that your lawn is mowed often and that bushes are trimmed. Adding flowers or flowering shrubs add color and interest and help keep your neighborhood attractive and the values up.

There are many magazines that carry helpful hints, plus Home and Garden TV and DIY networks show a lot of good ideas and how to do them. Home and Garden has wonderful shows that I love, such as "Curb Appeal." Remember, an attractive exterior is as important as a beautiful interior. FYI: this is true of your home as well as yourself. It only takes a few seconds for someone to form an opinion of you or your home. If people aren't attracted to your home's exterior, they might not want to see what the inside looks like when it is time to sell it. Right?

P.S. Anyone up for a block party? Our neighborhood has had several fun ones.

P.P.S. Treat others as you would like to be treated. Try harder to be sweet and nice – you can do it! I'm just not sure if this bad-ass bitch can!

Chapter 14 *Fun at the Gym*

Lordy, Lordy, Lordy, I signed up for gym membership. Since Curves closed I have been avoiding places like this for several years.

Curves had a circle of machines. You could use all or the ones you felt worked better for you. A workout could be done in thirty minutes – three times a week, I had a love/hate relationship with this routine. I loved that I lost weight and felt better without spending a lot of time. I also had fun with other gals. I hated that I had to do it! I didn't find nor have I ever found exercise fun. Well, maybe I did when I was thirty and played basketball once a week. Loved, loved, loved playing basketball but the timing sucked – seven to eight thirty in the evening. I was so "worked up" I had trouble getting to sleep.

Now I see that Curves is starting to advertise on television. I have a real problem with the people who started it. I don't feel the original owners of the franchise were fair to their franchises when the economy sank. I was told the franchise owners would not lower their fees. One owner who had two Curves facilities lost her businesses plus her home and cars. At sixty, she and her husband had to start all over. Another thirty-year-old owner told me she owed her parents over two hundred thousand dollars – very depressing. The other sixty or-so owner, I believe, was able to sell her building but lost a huge investment. About this time the franchise owners appeared on television and were seen getting into their private plane and flying to Texas, supposedly to help some poor folks in Houston. The television show said, I believe, they owned large acreage in the U.S. and South America. My question is if these owners were so bent on helping others, couldn't they lower their fees to help keep their businesses going? And what about all of us that were left stranded? There are a few Curves still in business here and there but not where I need them.

Back to the "new to me gym."

I do not like to look at or smell sweaty men, especially gray-haired old men in shorts with very hairy eyebrows, nose hair and armpit hair – ugh, ugh, ugh. I find the parking involves a lot of careful backing up to get in and out of the very crowded parking lot.

The set-up and type of machines are super different. Change isn't easy for old people – at least not for me.

I am NOT fond of exercise. However, I need to keep my balance, to try to keep fit and need to take off about twenty pounds Thus, I broke down and joined for one month. I decided to give it a try. Ugh, ugh, ugh! I went to a cardio – dance stretch – bar class (not the kind of bar I like to go to), lasting an hour. I am a competitive person. It is really hard on me to keep up with the very young Zumba type of fast moves. I did much better on the bar. The stretching involved floor exercises; I knew I couldn't get up without help, so forget it. This is how it was – loved the very fast music, though too fast for me, but not the early twenty-something, intense but sweet instructor. I noticed a hairy old man – mid-seventies – who was more obnoxious than he knew. He stood next to the instructor facing the music. He had leg muscles of a thirty-year-old guy. If you dressed him up in a suit he might have appeared to look normal. The instructor and the old guy faced the mirror with two class members, There were four more rows – I was in the back row, where I hoped not be noticed. The instructor would yell out things like, "Let's go – great day today!" as well as instructions like "left foot back for grapevine, turn to the left – kick, etc." These were generally repeated by "Old Guy." That just made him even more obnoxious and in addition, he was moving so fast he was not always in step. (Okay, it was my reaction to him.) Another guy, I noticed, was apparently new to this craziness. I believe he was/is a race car driver I met last year at physical rehab. (I believe this mid-fifties guy was getting over shoulder surgery.) I didn't get a chance to speak to him as I left when they started the mat/stretching.

I asked the sixty-something gal next to me how long she had been coming to this class. She told me a couple of months since she got through her treatment. (I took that to mean cancer treatment.) She was sweet and told me I would get better as time went on. Yeah, sure, I'm thinking, as I am not a coordinated person. Being that I try to look as nice as possible, I had an old well-fitting, not tight, longer knit top with a pair of white stretch – not tight – wider-legged pants, and plain gold-finished hoop earrings with old white leather sneakers. Another gal – late fifties – told me, "You are more dressed up than us." I told her I run errands after exercise. She said she did too. I said "The difference is, you look cute in your exercise clothes, I don't." Being tall and wearing white pants I felt like I "stood out" when I was trying to hide. I tried to keep up – sort of – as I did arm movements, taking some breaks to drink water.

Question is, dear God, is it too much for me to want to keep up and look good too? The next day I wasn't too sore, as I remember. I kind of cheated, so back to the gym I go to try another class. It was supposed to be easier. No way – the gal leading the class I'm guessing was in her mid-thirties – sweet, but when she got excited she raised her voice and it became very irritating to me. Guess what? Irritating hairy old man was there again in the front row – he was difficult to ignore. I tried the class for about ten minutes. Ugh – what else bothered me was this time the instructor had us go from left to left, to left, back to facing front. No way could I hide from her. It was too much for me.

Damn – I miss Curves.

I skipped a day and returned on Sunday afternoon of Labor Day weekend. I got the guys at the front desk to show me how to do one of the butt-ugly machines. Very few people were working out. I asked an older guy about a couple of other machines which I used for about five minutes. This guy looked to be in very good condition, but not like a thirty-year-old. He drives about forty miles to take advantage of the pool. He says warm water helps his arthritis. He was very nice, I'm guessing with a sweet wife at home.

A couple of days later I attended my first Tai Chi class. It looked so easy when I remember seeing it on television. Let me tell you, cookie – it isn't. An hour seems like a whole day. Slow movements done over and over make for tired muscles soon after and the next day. It made me aware of just how much I am out of shape.

As Oprah would say, "What I know for sure" is that "if you don't use it – you lose it." I hate to tell you but eating right and exercise need to be your highest priorities in life. I know people in assisted living or that are dead because of not taking care of themselves. If you don't want someone else wiping your butt, you better start taking care of yourself NOW!

Returning to Florida from our North Carolina home, I began an hour-long chair yoga class. I thought the first class would never end. I came home and took to my bed for an hour of rest. Now I generally feel good after the class. It is amazing in that you do feel it, working your body. I also go to a regular yoga class, do all the stand-up and then do chair yoga for the rest. I am also back doing Tai Chi once a week.

(Note to self: Quit being negative and just deal with it!) I do feel better.

You choose your own type of exercise, girlfriend.

P.S. In another words, get off your butt and just do it.

Chapter 15 *Fun Moving on to College*
This was a very special time for me.

If you have a son, daughter or grandchild going off to college I have some really good tips for y'all. These hints come from an article in The Ashville Citizen Times, written by Nancy Williams. It seems Nancy worked in housing for a college for almost thirty years. I was so impressed with the stuff I learned that I want to pass it on.

Nancy said college dorms have changed a lot since she went to school. Now you'll often find some with snack bars, movie theaters as well as computer labs and shocking, but yes – double beds.

Do you think they might even have condom machines? I'm just trying to be realistic. Nancy said it is often possible to get a cleaning service. Question: Don't kids need to learn to clean up after themselves? If you haven't taught them how to do laundry, iron a shirt and pair of pants, mend a hem or clean a bathroom you need to do so NOW, or ask your household helper to teach them. They may have a time later on in life when they actually need to care for themselves. That includes cooking simple meals, including cleaning up as they go and how to dust and run a vacuum.

Don't they need to learn how to handle credit cards and checking accounts?

Before your child leaves home for college, he or she will probably be provided with a list of necessary items and the name and e-mail of their roommate. It is important for the kids to work out who might bring a mini-vacuum, etc. Don't load up on non-necessary items. They will need sheets. A matching comforter and draperies are attractive but a lot of kids make do with what they have used in high school and others like to coordinate with their roommates. Some items such as toilet paper may be purchased a few rolls at a time. Dorm storage is often quite small. Something to remember, who needs a blender? A thermometer, duct tape and an inexpensive flash light could come in handy. Then just add a pillow and a blanket. But, seriously, your child can pick up anything else on campus or order them from Amazon.

Things to beware of, according to Nancy's article, are the companies and manufacturers trying to sell you a lot of unnecessary stuff.

Caution your child about locking his door. Lots of stuff "walks off" from those who don't do this. Electronics and televisions could be very tempting and very expensive to replace.

I would advise your child that sharing a room won't be easy. If he or she uses more than their space they won't win the "popularity" award. As difficult as it is for the student, sometimes it is harder on the parent. I missed our sons when they moved on with their lives, but was happy that I had taught them a good many life skills and lessons. They and our only grandson could cook a good meal, clean and iron a shirt and could clean. I should have helped them with managing money. Now I'm proud to say they are all doing well in life. Maybe I helped them get there. I do know I am very proud of each of them.

If you are a parent that is really unsettled by it all – take up a new hobby, get out of the house and don't interfere with your child's life. I actually know one mom who called her kid's professor. It may not be easy to let your kid go but if you have done your job well, you should be able to trust your child.

Put them in God's hands, pray and let go. Okay?

P.S. You may have to pray a lot. (I feel sorry for those that haven't learned how to do this yet.)

Chapter 16 *Fun With Car Guys*

You know how I love to chat and yes, tend to give guys a rough time. I met Deli Guy at an Ingles grocery store in North Carolina. He is a nice looking older man. (No, I didn't say handsome.) He has a friendly face and manner as he waits on the old bitches, like me. He clearly loves people. I would see him about once a week when I would pick up a couple of items from the deli usually on Monday evenings after our Watching Our Weight (WOW) group meeting. When he wasn't busy we would talk for a few minutes. I would ask him, "How are you doing today?" He would crack me up by saying, "I'm just living the good life." I gave him one of my bookmarks and told him that *Hold On To Your Panties And Have Fun* makes a good gift for fun women. He said he thought his wife would enjoy reading it. I told him he could get it at the local bookstore in Franklin.

One time Deli Guy and I were discussing older people and age in general. He said, "I'm probably a lot older than you." I looked at his full head of white hair and sparkling eyes and replied, "I don't think so. How old are you?" He replied, "Seventy-four." I told him, "I'm eighty, I just look better." He was laughing as I went on my way.

Months later Deli Guy and I got to talking about cars. I love, love, love beautiful sports cars! It is my favorite guy topic. He told me he just sent his 1991 BMW sports car to auto heaven with four hundred, sixty three thousand miles on it! No accidents, no dings and no dents. He told me he had bought it new and had paid cash for it. I replied, "That's an amazing story! Enquiring minds want to know, how much it cost you." "As I remember I paid twenty-seven thousand dollars, cash." "Enquiring minds want to know how you had that much money saved." Deli Guy went on to tell me that he had been a mid-weight prizefighter for sixteen years. I said, "Gosh, I thought you were smart." He must have been good to still have his wits about him and not have a smashed-in face, right? Then I asked him what car replaced the BMW. He replied, "A Ford Taurus." I told him I drove one as a loaner. When the owner of the dealership asked me how I liked it, I replied, "It's an Old Fart's car." Deli Guy grinned as another customer approached the deli counter. What a fun guy! Questions I still hope to ask him: How did he get from prizefighting to Ingles Deli? Multiple marriages? To get out of the house?? Or to hang out with cool people like me – ha, ha.

Recently, Hubby and I were watching "Jay Leno's Garage." Jay told this charming story. A lady in her early nineties called him up and asked him if he would be interested in a car she and her husband had purchased new in 1951. The Hudson Hornet had been sitting in her garage since her husband's death several years earlier. Jay went to see the car. The ninety-two-year-old lady, who looked to be in her seventies, was out in the garage with her little duster cleaning it off. She asked Jay if he might want to buy it. He asked how much she wanted for it. She replied, "$5,000." He wrote her a check. It took a while but Jay had it completely re-done. I got the impression Jay farmed out some of the work and did the rest himself. When it was done, four or five years later, Jay decided to try to call this lady – not knowing if she was still alive. She was. He asked her if she wanted to see the car and go for a ride in it. She said she had to get her hair done, etc., etc. She also wanted to bring her kids along. Jay agreed. This lady's boys were, I believe, seventy-two and seventy-four. The sons got into an argument over something related to riding in their old car. Their Mama turned around, yelling at them and smacked them like they were teenagers.

Some Mamas never change!

P.S. Note to my sons and grandson – Aren't you lucky I don't haul off and hit you?

Chapter 17 Fun With Sweet Tees and Sweet Dreams

I like T-shirts on guys with abs, how about you? I also like to see any T-shirt neat and clean.

From time to time I have received gifts from "Catalog Favorites." Not one of the gag gifts, but a lovely jacket and top I really like. The prices are moderate, the quality very good. I don't wear tees with printing of any kind but how I love the creative sayings. How about, "FROM NOW ON WE ARE SCREWING THINGS UP MY WAY." Wouldn't you love to say that to your boss?

Do you like, "A WISE MAN ONCE SAID, 'I'LL ASK MY WIFE'"? Or maybe, "RETIRED AND DOWN TO ONE BOSS, MY WIFE"? I love, "IF A MAN SAYS HE WILL FIX IT, THERE IS NO NEED TO REMIND HIM EVERY SIX MONTHS." Hey, Hubby, how do you like this one? "ONCE IN AWHILE SOMEONE AMAZING COMES ALONG, HERE I AM"! And baby, I have been here a LONG time! You know we both can identify with, "YOUNG AT HEART, SLIGHTLY OLDER IN OTHER PLACES." Okay, what about, "I CAN EXPLAIN IT TO YOU BUT I CAN'T UNDERSTAND IT FOR YOU"? Another I identify with, sort of, is "BEING KNOWN AS THE FUN ONE OF THE GROUP IS A GOOD THING, UNLESS YOU'RE IN PRISON."

Do you like the little kids' tees that have such cute sayings like, "WHAT'S THIS 'NO' WORD YOU SPEAK OF?" It comes in pink or blue from www.catalogfavorites.com. I also like,

"DADS KNOW A LOT BUT GRANDPAS KNOW EVERYTHING," or at least they think they do, right? This catalog also has fun license tags and plaques. For instance, "UNCLE, LIKE A DAD ONLY COOLER." They have team products and inspirational items, and even a nice tee, "WHEN LIFE GETS TOO HARD TO STAND, KNEEL." I agree.
The company that prints these tees seems to be an equal opportunity company in that they also have the following, "LEAD ME NOT INTO TEMPTATION... OH HELL JUST FOLLOW ME I KNOW A SHORTCUT."

Another has a crown and says, "THE QUEEN OF ABSOLUTELY EVERYTHING." Wonder if it was written by someone that has met me? Ha, ha. I wonder if you love this one: "I COULD BE A MORNING PERSON, IF MORNING HAPPENED AT NOON." That is definitely me! "I'M

AWESOME DON'T QUESTION IT JUST DEAL WITH IT."
That isn't me, sweetheart. "THE LAKE IS CALLING AND I
MUST GO" could be my daughter-in-law. "DON'T GET ME
STARTED. I DON'T HAVE BRAKES" is me, isn't it?

How about this? Get together for a "Girl's Night" with your
best friends, perhaps some margaritas, and make up your own
sayings. Everyone gets matching, maybe pink printed tee for
your next get-together, road trip or beach trip? Wouldn't that
be fun?

P.S. Two of my personal favorites: "YOU CAN'T BUY
HAPPINESS BUT YOU CAN BUY BOOKS" and "IT DOESN'T
MATTER IF MY GLASS IS HALF EMPTY OR HALF FULL,
CLEARLY THERE IS ROOM FOR MORE WINE IN IT." So
true!

Fun Getting To Sweet Dreams

As digestion revs up our metabolism we need to have big
meals early in the evening.

Take a hot bath or shower. This will produce a drop in
your body temperature and should produce a deeper and
longer sleep.

Put on a pair of socks as they warm you and become a
natural sedative. Try listening to slow soothing music for
about forty-five to sixty minutes. Stay away from MSG as it can
cause sleep problems. To decrease waking in the middle of the
night, try to get to bed thirty minutes earlier than you normally
do.

Set your radio or light-simulating device to wake you
instead of an alarm clock with a loud blast. Don't get into the
habit of going to sleep with the TV. Watch your alcohol intake.
For example, more than two glasses of wine will cause you to
go to sleep faster but you will wake up more often.

Experts say if you wake up you should get up and read for a while.

Avoid staying stimulated by electronics including your smart phone. Turn off the television and all electronic items at least one hour before bedtime.

Don't consume caffeine after two or three p.m.

Get yourself into a bedtime routine. Brush and floss your teeth, shower, etc. Have a note pad on your night stand to write down stuff you will need to do the next day.

Keep a grateful diary to write down all the good things that happened that day. This will make you a more positive person as well as relax you.

Turn off your light and say your prayers. P.S. Sweet Dreams!

Chapter 18 Fun With Good Friends

My friend Betty reminds me of Betty Boop with her great big blue eyes and round smiling face.

When I saw her at TOPS (Taking Off Pounds Successfully) I would say, "Hi, Betty Boop." She told me her uncle had called her "Betty Boop" as well. When I saw a Betty Boop hat, I just had to get it for her.

Betty grew up in the Midwest in the thirties and forties. She had several younger brothers and a sister. Her mom died when she was fourteen. Her dad expected her to do all the household work and take care of her younger siblings. When she was sixteen she met a sailor at a dance. They were soon married. They moved to "Paradise Island" where her husband got a good job at the paper mill, eventually moving into management of some sort. They had three children, two sons and a daughter. One son died at seventeen in a tragic car accident. Her husband retired and loved spending time with his family who remained in the area. He loved fishing, golf and (according to our mutual friend Gail) having sex with his wife while it was raining. Gail told me, in front of Betty, that "once the phone was off the hook..." And Betty laughed! Two years into retirement, her husband was diagnosed with cancer. He died two years later. This was before I met Betty. Years later her son had cancer. It was serious. He died about three years after diagnosis. Betty's strong Catholic faith got her through all the crap.

Betty was blessed to have a wonderful daughter and talented grandkids who were known locally as good bright fun children. I knew her granddaughter who was a local pharmacist. I met her daughter's husband and Betty's great grandkids during visiting hours at the funeral home – truly a wonderful sweet family.

At some time during her life Betty had her breasts removed, cancer. She always struggled to keep her weight down. She was a short gal who was probably forty to fifty pounds overweight. Betty was taking meds for heart problems. In spite of all of this, Betty always had a smile on her face and time for her friends and her church.

As the years went on Betty complained of on-going knee pain. She saw a specialist who said both knees needed to be replaced. Her daughter didn't think she should due to her age (mid-eighties). Her heart surgeon didn't feel her heart was strong enough so she suffered on. Once in a while she would make the effort to go out for lunch. Her pharmacist granddaughter began to check on her every day.

I was in North Carolina when I heard she was in the hospital. She had cancer in her chest. The doctor wanted to do surgery

– she refused and went back to her cute white cottage with the sky blue trim.

I understand Betty's daughter died about a week before she died. Not sure if Betty was told or not.

What a sad, sad life in that she lost her husband and all her children, before she died, as well as her best friend of over sixty years – Gail.

As I mentioned, Gail was also a friend of mine although I felt closer to Betty. While Betty was a "salt of the earth" gal who looked nice in her casual clothes – Gail was a fashion-forward gal. She was into shoes, bags, jewelry and very fashionable clothes. Gail and Betty met soon after World War II when they both moved to Paradise Island. Their husbands both worked at "the mill." Gail was pregnant and Betty had her first-born son who was just a baby. They soon became best friends. I know Gail had several miscarriages, plus, I believe, a still-born. Gail was Baptist. I think she had a son and a daughter.

Almost everyone experiences losses in their lives; Gail's were very traumatic. Her teenage son fell to his death from a highflying carnival ride, according to Betty. This was, of course, long before I met Gail and her husband.

Gail had a delightful personality. She was outgoing and pleasant but a bit of a mischief-maker. She loved to push Betty's buttons. If you have known someone sixty-plus years – you know how to do this. It was all done with love and humor. Gail had traveled more than Betty, so was a bit worldlier. She colored her hair while Betty's was pure white. Betty was a much better driver. Betty and I gave Gail a rough time about her lack of parking ability (usually three to four feet from the curb.) I believe Gail went to TOPS, for social reasons. At one time I think she was ten to fifteen pounds over. What was amazing to me was before weighing in, Gail would remove all her rings, bracelets and earrings! Although "good stuff," they couldn't have weighed that much. She always wore the same size clothes during the fifteen years I knew her.

I believe Gail had heart issues but it was kidney failure that "got her." She had dialysis for a while then decided to stop that. She died peacefully at home holding her Bible, surrounded by her family.

Now Gail and Betty are together again. And I love that. How I miss those gals.

P.S. Why did I tell you sad stories? Maybe because you might realize how precious life is. When you have some crappy times in life you will realize it could be worse.

Chapter 19 Fun With My Ohio Family

Our phone rang. It was my sister. It was late afternoon the day after Thanksgiving. She told me our only brother, Larry, our only other sibling had died. The funeral was to be the next day, one thousand miles away.

This brought back a flood of memories. My first memory of my brother was as a handsome baby in his crib. He, like me, was born in our paternal grandparents' home. No doubt delivered by the same female physician who had delivered me. At that time I was about twenty months old and apparently bored so I amused myself by wadding up toilet paper and pushing it in the keyholes in this five-bedroom Victorian Craftsman home. Our father was a supervisor for a large Civilian Conservation Corps camp. The Depression-era program was set up by President Franklin Roosevelt. This group of men were put to work helping to build bridges and roads. Our very bright dad had graduated from the OSU, in Agricultural Engineering.

At this time we lived in Coshocton, Ohio. I remember my brother and me playing house and his favorite, cowboys and Indians. We played with a boy about our age and sometimes this boy would let us drive his fire truck. We both wanted one like it. My brother was five and I six and a half when our younger sister was born. She was very important to my brother and me. I had prayed and prayed for a little sister. I was bored playing cowboys and Indians. My brother was always "the cowboy," like Roy Rogers or Gene Autry. I wanted a little sister to play "house" and "school" with me. My next memory was of my brother and me walking to and from school. He was in first grade, I in second. Our mother told me to take care of and watch out for him. I'm not sure how far we lived from school, probably not far. (Our mother was a good mother, but I wouldn't have let my boys walk to school alone.) We moved to Martinsville, Ohio, when I was nine and a half, my brother almost eight. We took the bus to and from school. Seemingly it took a long time, to drop off the other kids before we got home. When my brother was ten, we would ride our bikes in good weather. During this time we both had chores. Mine was gathering the eggs, weeding, dusting the furniture, baseboards and the wooden stair steps. I also helped with washing and drying dishes. (This was long before dishwashers.) My brother helped our dad with farm work. In spite of our chores we still had some time to play. We would often tie one end of a clothesline to the gate and take turns jumping rope. We loved playing with our kittens, even teaching them to do tricks. We set up a ladder for the kittens in the wash house. (This was a separate building next to the house, which our great-grandparents had used for washing. This small building had been the original house on the property.) My dad told us his grandmother, Nancy, would heat water in the fireplace, place it in a big tub and wash the clothes by hand using a washboard. Then she would wring out the clothes by hand. By the time we lived there, Mother had a wringer-washer. It had a motor agitator that would swirl the clothes. Then you would have to stop the washer and put the wash, piece by piece, through the wringer. The clothes would be lifted into another big tub of rinse water. You would swirl the clothes with a long stick, then put them through the wringer again. At that point they would be ready to hang on the clothesline.

I remember hanging a piece of clothing and seeing it freeze before I could hang out the next piece if we didn't have room to hang on lines in the wash house. During the winter we placed small pieces on a wooden folding rack if the weather was bad.

Our home had a big furnace in which coal was burned, producing ashes. My brother and I carried the ashes from the furnace outside. The ashes formed into a large pile near our vegetable garden, which I believe Daddy worked into the soil to make it richer.

The basement had stone walls and a dirt floor. Outside were a few steps that went down to a door to the inside. We also had stairs to the main part of the house. Eggs were kept in the cool basement. I gathered the eggs, then once a week my brother and I would clean them with a damp cloth. While cleaning the eggs, we would chat. After a while it could get very boring. I picked up a cracked egg. I remember thinking it would be a cool thing to throw. I said, "Catch." He wasn't ready so it hit him on his forehead and dripped down his face. To a ten-and-a-half-year-old this was very funny. To the nine-year-old who was hit, not so funny. He started after me as I ran up the stairs yelling, "Mother, Mother, save me!" I'm sure I was disciplined. From then on we cleaned them at the kitchen table under Mother's supervision. No, it wasn't nice of me, but ten-year-olds do stupid stuff. From what I hear, it's not unusual for brothers and sisters to do stuff like this. I can still remember the shock on his face and sadly – I still think it was funny. My brother was probably jealous he didn't think of doing that to me first.

While we lived in the Martinsville community during World War II, our dad, my brother and I collected milk pods from weeds along our fences. We were told they would be used to make into parachutes. At that time the government had rationing. It restricted our buying of shoes, clothes, sugar, flour, meat, etc. Mother saved coupons for our flour and sugar so she could make cakes and cookies for truly important occasions like birthdays and Christmas.

I was given a lot of responsibility in caring for our little sister. We all spoiled her, and my brother and I probably overprotected her. We thought she was "so special" because she was very sweet and when small was a bit shy. I was responsible for dressing her, etc. I almost became her second mother.

After our grandfather died, my grandmother wanted her younger son to move to the farm. Our parents bought a sixty-eight-acre farm about thirty-five miles away. Our dad and our brother farmed it. We girls helped in the house and garden. I sometimes mowed the yard, which was nearly an acre, with an old-fashioned push mower, when my brother was busy birthing pigs and sheep or working in the fields. My brother and I had pigs and sheep as 4-H projects. We also had a couple of beef cows. One of them was butchered for our meat and the other sold. We had a large freezer for storing meat. Mother canned beef for soup, etc. In addition Mother canned tomatoes, beans, peas, etc., from our garden. Farming is a very hard way to make a living.

My brother would go to school and then come home to take care of all the animals. When it was time to put in or harvest crops, Dad would use vacation time. He and Larry worked very hard. My brother was taken out of school. Fortunately he, like his sisters, was very smart. (Ha ha). Actually, he was smarter than I and had the gift of a photographic mind while I had the gift of gab. When we were in high school and were in Latin class together, he would look at the vocabulary words once and remember them forever. I worked very hard to keep up with him.

When Mother was forty she learned to drive. I was sixteen, my brother fifteen, and sister ten. At this time our dad decided to go back to government work. He worked as a soil conservation agent in a county about fifty miles away. Eventually our dad moved to Fayette County where we lived. Later he received a lifetime award for his services. This was helping farmers plan proper drainage in order to make their land more productive. He also taught them about crop rotation to help them reap even better harvests.

With Dad away during the week, most of the farm responsibility fell on our brother. I felt this was unfair, but I guess our dad didn't feel he had a choice. When the sheep were having their lambs, Larry would sleep in our modern concrete barn. I believe he had a sleeping bag and a heater of some sort.

Other memories of my brother and sister are the fun times we had as a family. We played cards or listened to radio shows. We didn't have television until I was seventeen and it was black and white. My brother and I were always competitive yet loved to joke with one another. Though I didn't think it was

funny when I was thirteen and he often called me "FAT ASS."
I was at the time developing curves, had pimples, new glasses
and ugly corrective shoes. However, I never could stay angry
with him as he was always making our family laugh.

One of the things my brother prided himself on was that
he could guess what his gifts were before he opened them.
When we were teenagers I decided I would put a "stop" to that,
and I did. I got a box and a lot of newspaper, and since he loved
baked beans I got him a huge can about ten inches tall. The box
I put them in was about thirty inches tall. I added a couple of
bricks, a Coke can filled with pennies, and the beans, then
added a brick. The box weighed a lot. The pennies and bolts
rattled. I put it under the tree a week or so before Christmas.
He would shake it every time he was near the tree. He couldn't
figure it out. That fun gift made my holiday! In our family we
never gave big gifts but we tried to make them fun, perhaps
some small items such as a couple of their favorite candy bars.
Sometimes we would make something for them. Our mother
would make my sister and me matching dresses. A few times
when I was young Aunt Emily would buy me a dress, one being
a "Shirley Temple" dress. I never had store-bought clothes
except for underwear and sweaters until I saved up money and
bought a two-piece bright orange sleeveless blouse and
matching skirt when I was college age. The top had rhinestone
buttons down the front with stitched pleats. The skirt had
small pleats. It was a real bitch to iron. My mother hated it as
she thought the buttons and color made it tacky. As much as
my mother hated it, I loved it. I kept wearing it until I was
about twenty-five.

Many years later when my brother turned seventy-five,
I sent him about fifteen kinds of beans. All of these I wrapped
separately. It cost about twenty-five dollars for postage alone...

He sent me a really funny poem that he wrote about how much he enjoyed the beans and the farts, too. This poem, I believe, was the only correspondence he ever sent me. (Christmas cards were signed by his wife.) I would call him for his birthdays.

My brother, sister and I were very active in community organizations such as 4-H, high school band and choir. Larry and I were always county winners in the academic school tests we took. I was sixteenth in the state in biology. I also was outstanding 4-H girl in Fayette County when I was sixteen, having completed twenty-four projects in eight years. I remember winning the county public speaking contest. The seven dollars I won was awesome. WOW! I earned money talking. Not sure what my brother or sister won, but know they won their share. Larry was very charismatic and fun to be around. He was elected class president and was also valedictorian.

My bother loved to hunt. I guess he learned how from our Uncle Dick (Mother's much younger brother.) Our dad didn't really approve. After college I worked about thirty miles away from my parents' house. My brother, then twenty-one, went hunting with his best friend. They were cleaning their guns, which they thought were unloaded. My brother was accidentally hit in the knee. Thank God he was a bright guy who loved to read. He told his friend to take his belt off and make a tourniquet to stop the bleeding. Long story short, he lost his knee. The surgeon had to fuse the two bones together (since this was long before artificial knees). My brother came home to heal and was in bed close to a year. Our mother rose to the occasion and provided the best of nursing care. My brother met Bev, a sweet, cute radiologist assistant, while in the hospital. He looked forward to her frequent visits. He was determined to get on with his life as he married Bev, the love of his life.

Our parents and hers must have done a lot to help them out. It couldn't have been easy for them. Dad made a decent living, but there were not funds for a lot of extras.

I had been working part-time to pay for my books and clothes while going to college. About this time my mother told me I would have to pay back all the money for my tuition. She said they would pay my room and board, but needed the tuition money back so my sister could go to college. (It took me five years but I did pay them back.)

Larry had completed a business correspondence class I had told him about. A year after their marriage, my brother and his wife welcomed a baby boy, and a few years later they had two baby girls.

When their oldest son was about three, Beverly's parents brought Bev and their son to Clearwater. While her parents were off visiting others. Bev and their son stayed with us. Our oldest was four, and our youngest, one. We had a lovely time together. Larry stayed in Ohio to work.

I don't think I saw them again until we flew to Ohio for our sister's wedding. His daughters and our youngest son were about kindergarten age. We enjoyed seeing everyone.

The summer after we had moved to the Atlanta area from California, when my boys were about six and nine, I drove from Georgia to Ohio to see my family. My mother, my two sons and I went to my brother's for a family picnic. When we arrived Bev was setting up the food. I was told to go to the house to get my brother. I knocked on the door. When he came out, I said," What a cute beer belly!" My brother EXPLODED!!! I honestly had never seen ANYONE that mad!

He got in his truck and peeled off, only to come back later after I thought he had calmed down. I told him I was sorry I had upset him and apologized to his wife and kids. I was surprised he got that mad because he called me "FAT ASS" for YEARS! My mother wanted to know what happened. I told her. She said he reacted that way because he was so against drinking. I had apparently woken him up and I agree that wasn't what I should have said.

Skip forward to Thanksgiving weekend 2013. Our kids, now in their fifties, were visiting. Friday afternoon they took off to do some Christmas shopping. I had a few minutes to call my sister to check in on her and see how her Thanksgiving turned out. (She lost her husband the Thanksgiving before.) I left a message as she was not home. Late Friday afternoon she called back and told me my brother had died on Monday. The funeral was to be the next afternoon in southern Ohio. I was in Florida, a thousand miles away. (Apparently my brother had nine different medical problems.) She told me she had gone to see him in October for his birthday and that he was in very poor shape. Supposedly he asked her not to tell me. Later that afternoon, my family was back. I told them about my brother's death. My youngest told me that when he was six and we were visiting, while playing with his cousins he had climbed up on top of a dresser. He said he shouldn't have. My son went on to say that my brother pulled off his belt and beat him. I had blocked this out of my mind. I told my son I was so sorry. My heart ached for him. He certainly deserved to be disciplined but not with a belt. Our grandfather, our dad's father, was known to be a hot-head at times. While I remember a couple of spankings I never knew of any belt beatings in our home.

I believed my brother took his anger at me out on my son. Thinking about this I finally remembered T.J. crying. I should have checked his body. I remember my mother being upset and us leaving. I never went back there and that was probably why. Yet, my brother and I went on to share some very special brother/sister moments. Whenever I drove to Ohio and was visiting my mother and dad, my brother would drive about thirty miles, one way, to see me. We saw each other at our parents' fiftieth anniversary party and again at our parents' funerals. We were always good with retorts going back and forth and this continued as we aged.

The funeral was the next day. Needless to say, I couldn't go. Over the years I have tried to reach out to his children several times. Apparently all they remember is seeing their dad very angry the day of the picnic. I had a friend message the funeral home site for me. I would have certainly tried to be a good aunt given the opportunity. Sadly I didn't even have a chance to send flowers.

It was a horrible shock to hear of my brother's passing. I was not made aware of his declining health, nor of his death until it was too late. Although he and I were not close, he still was my only brother. This was very difficult for me. Very sad as I had loved my brother. I feel my sister could have kept me informed; however my sister is a very complex person. While I love her I don't understand her. Although we were raised by the same parents we look at life and other people differently. My sister followed me to the OSU and went on to be an extension agent for the OSU. She married an OSU graduate who worked out of their home. They bought a nice-sized farm and grew fruits and vegetables. They were known for their great strawberries. They had three sons in three years. Interestingly, their birthdays are all the same week. My sister took over managing the direct sale of the produce. Their home life always seemed hectic. To me, it seemed like a madhouse during strawberry seasons. People would be knocking on the door and the phone ringing off the hook. (I probably made it worse by visiting at that time of year.) I have always been impressed with her management skills.

My sister and her husband did a great job of raising three sons. One is a sales manager, one a Mohs cancer surgeon and the other is finishing his PhD as he teaches college classes in China. Apparently these boys have made wonderful parents and marriage partners. My sister started them off with her own preschool. When they got older the boys picked produce and were given money toward their college expenses. Her husband, one of the boys recalled at his dad's funeral, did not allow roughhousing in the house. If they were caught they had to run laps around the outside of the house, regardless of rain, sleet or snow. I wish Hubby and I had thought of that cool idea. A great way for kids to run off excess energy.

When my sister's kids were, I believe, college age my sister taught high school. My sister and her husband had a good life until her husband's health began to decline. He had a twelve-year battle with Parkinson's disease. After being diagnosed with a rare spinal disorder that causes one to faint and fall backward, my sister is now living at home with caregivers. Fortunately, she can afford in her home care. The last twenty years have not been the life I would have chosen for her. I try to remember that we are told in the Bible, "Judge not lest ye be judged." I love and care about my sister even though I often don't understand her. I thank God she and I often talk on the phone and that I got to visit with her when in Ohio a couple of years ago. I also thank God I seem to have good relationships with her sons.

When thinking about my Ohio family I remember all of us working together and the fun we had when we weren't working. Even though my dad was brought up by Quaker Victorian parents, we had parents who hugged and weren't afraid to kiss each other in front of us. They always provided a united front when we kids messed up. My dad learned to have fun after meeting my mother's amusing brothers and sisters. The only time I remember him ever saying no to our mother was when she wanted to work at the floral shop. Apparently the florist had seen her award-winning floral designs. My dad could do anything professionally; however, he didn't want his wife working. That was heartbreaking for our mother.

My Dad and Mother were both very outgoing, attractive and fun. I need to tell you two things about "my Daddy." He drove fifty miles one way to pick me up and another fifty miles to take me back to the OSU the next day so I could vote. What made him a super Dad was that I voted for Eisenhower while he voted for Stevenson. Mother and Dad always voted though; one was a Democrat and the other a Republican. I never heard them argue about politics. This is probably why I am an Independent. Another thing I learned from my Dad is to be forgiving. I know he prided himself on getting a guy to say "hi" to him by crossing the street so he would "run into" the guy who didn't like him. (I never heard of anyone else who didn't like him.)

I was blessed with Christian parents and a brother and sister who seemed to love me most of the time. Our kids all became good citizens with loving families of their own. We tried to stay in touch and had good times when we got together.

Chapter 20 Fun In Georgia and Florida

Hubby got a job offer he couldn't refuse in Atlanta, Georgia. We lived in Tucker and then Roswell for about forty years. During this time, I spent as much time in the Clearwater, Florida, area as possible. I was very allergic to Georgia's dropping temperatures especially with dampness and mildew.

My allergies produced severe sinus migraines that would go on for days; in fact, a day without a headache was to be celebrated. The job situation was horrible! I was "let go" from one teaching position because I wasn't able to take a second graduate class in one year. (Unfortunately, I was an example.) Another teaching job, I was "let go" along with several other really good teachers. The reason given was one of my students, the only daughter after five boys, was unhappy with me because I didn't let her sit where she wanted. I know this sounds ridiculous but her parents ran the school. Had I gone to NEA about it, I probably could have gotten my job back. A lot of the parents, I found out later, thought I was the best teacher their child had in six years. I could have, but didn't fight it, as by the end of the year I had gained twenty pounds and had a stomach ulcer.

It was a heartbreaking experience. Adding to that was the heartbreak of a lack of support from my Hubby. After a six week break I went to work for a job placement agency. I loved it until the company was bought out by another company. The new owners were former owners of a collection agency; it wasn't the same. Even though I did well sales-wise, I was "too much" for these guys. Meaning, a strong Northern personality was not what strong Southern men wanted.

My next position was as a decorator for a lighting/paint and wallpaper place. I worked with builders and loved it. However, after six months, at Christmas time, I was let go. (A pink slip in my pay check.) I found out when I opened my pay envelope. I nearly fainted. I was crushed again!

Three times in a year! The economy was the reason in this case.

Shortly, I found a job at J.C. Penney's in the decorating department. I didn't like working so many evenings but overall liked the job. The problem was their ineffective workroom. Being creative I designed and sold a big job that involved swags and long jabos on either side of sheers for a formal living room. As a result of the workroom screwing it up, the client cancelled the entire job. They had planned a party and the job wasn't done correctly. Unfortunately, I quit Penney's without having another job. I met another designer fresh out of design school who had been working there with me at the same time. He left shortly afterwards and started his own business. I tried working with him but we both struggled to make any money. About this time a Clearwater friend, another Dalmatian breeder, talked me into working in her lovely design shop in Clearwater. My friend carried all the major expensive furniture brands, such as Henredon, La Barge (glass and brass), plus top drapery and upholstery fabrics and wonderful wallpapers. Since she was the busiest in the winter and a friend, I was able to spend time in Clearwater and Roswell. However, it didn't work out quite like I expected. Her husband at the time couldn't cope with two similar personalities. I felt he took advantage of her, coming in late and not putting in his fair share of time and effort in the business. I left due to his attitude and because I found a better position.

I loved making more money, a base plus commission, and loved that the new company advertising brought in more sales. It was a much larger store in a better location; however, it became more difficult to get to Roswell and spend time with my husband and older son. The younger one had come to Florida with me. It wasn't easy for Hubby to get time off work to come to Florida. (He worked eight to five – then home for dinner and then back to work for another three hours on Mondays through Thursdays, with a regular day on Fridays and four to five hours on Saturdays.) This schedule went on for about ten years. When Hubby had to go into the hospital for a heart check and our oldest moved out of the house, I decided that if I was going to save our marriage, I needed to move back to Roswell. At that point, I went to work for a "for profit" college. One of the ways they make lots of money is paying the teachers a low hourly wage and charging the students high tuition. It is supposed to be a prestigious thing to work at these schools. Because I had previous experience gaining certifications for high schools, I was hired by the Atlanta School of Art and Interior Design. I enjoyed the students; unfortunately I had to put in lots of extra hours for which I wasn't rewarded. I was asked to teach a class on advertising. I told them I knew nothing about advertising. They said it wouldn't be a problem as I was an excellent teacher. I was advised to just keep ahead of the students. Boy, did I ever learn a lot. When I was told there would be no summer income as there were not enough summer students, I went to another for profit school, Patricia Stevens. This school started in New York as a modeling school. I taught all the interior design classes, classes on how to dress, fabric types and uses, etc. I liked my job, except for the money. After a year the owner's wife, who had been in my classes, took over teaching them. "We're so sorry but we don't have enough classes for you both."

My experiences for the most part were positive. I loved the young people and enjoyed the classes. It was the feeling of being taken advantage of that hurt – a lot! In between and during these jobs I did some interior design work; I also did some interesting part-time work that didn't pay well, but it helped pay for our groceries and the dog expenses. One of my part- time jobs was doing market research. I interviewed people for food brand preferences, soap, and the most interesting – one apparently paid for by the French Government – on travel. This involved me calling people and setting up appointments at their homes or businesses. One interview took about an hour. I had no problem meeting my quotas as people love to talk about their travel experiences. I met an Atlanta premier hair dresser and interviewed him while he did a gorgeous cut, color and style on a gal from Birmingham, Alabama. Interesting to me was that she came monthly to get her hair done. I loved the market research but it didn't bring in much money. To be a fulltime person you needed a degree in Marketing. This company called me when they needed me. If I was able to help them, I did.

When I was almost fifty I decided to open my own shop in Roswell. I called it "The Strawberry Unicorn." I had antiques, art and interior design. I had taken the retired businessman's course on starting a business and studied books on business. I remember reading that successful antique shops are next to or near other antique shops. My business was not. BIG MISTAKE! I gave up the business because I wasn't doing well financially or health wise. I had cancer, stage one. I was very fortunate in that surgery was all they suggested. I heard of an MD – a woman in Tucker, Georgia, who was very good in recommending herbs and vitamins.

During my four-hour surgery I believe Hubby really became concerned about me. He suggested that we buy a small cottage north of Clearwater in Palm Harbor, Florida. I had a lot of fun decorating it with super finds from used furniture and antique stores. I also enjoyed working in the yard doing landscaping. During this time I did some part-time work and my dog had a couple of litters of puppies. We had this house for about four years; however, the expense of my three weeks; hospital stay (kidney failure) meant we had to sell the house. Once again I had no choice but to return to Roswell. I loved being in Florida and loved the location. It was tough.

My main source of fun in Georgia was showing my dogs and meeting people. While I loved my Hubby and boys, it was difficult for me to cope with job problems, keeping a large home and our boys' growing independence. I was active in the American Association of University Women and the Atlanta Kennel Club. Hubby and I were founding members of the Dalmatian Club of Greater Atlanta. We had many dog meetings and parties at our home, which were always fun.

P.S. Why did I tell you all this negative stuff? There are lots of people who go through crap in their lives but get through it. Life goes on so you can focus on the negatives or you can make your life easier or better. The choice is yours.

Chapter 21 *Fun With Family Reunions*

Recently, I read an article on how to plan and host a family reunion. It got me to thinking and remembering our family reunions, or should I say, my grandparents. Armasia and Chloe Cleland were my paternal grandparents and Quakers (a religious group that believes in God and the simple, not materialistic life). Their friends were church members and neighbors. They were very bright, hardworking people who loved their family, though were not demonstrative.

Every summer a Sunday afternoon was set aside for a big family reunion. The location varied but was often held at my grandparents' farm. This involved lots of old people (my parents and grandparents' ages) sitting around talking. Usually, the only children present were my younger brother and sister, our first cousins, a son and daughter of my dad's younger brother and his wife, both also younger. (I was the oldest grandchild on either side of our family.)

We had more fun when my cousins' twenty-something aunt would come and play with us. We all adored her. The main event was dinner, consisting of fried chicken and summer vegetables with several desserts. It was good simple food, except for the chocolate cake or pies Mother usually made. She loved cooking and baking. She was much better at it than my grandma. (Sidebar: Maybe I have gotten my lack of interest in cooking from this grandma.) I enjoyed these get-togethers but have no real fond memories of them. I, being the oldest kid, didn't fit in with the younger ones or the adults.

My maternal grandparents' family reunions were always more joyous. My grandparents, Frank and Ada Zurbuch had five living children. Again I was the oldest of the cousins; however, I had an aunt who was ten years older and an uncle about eight years older. I hung out with them. My Aunt Emily was older but always had time for me. She and her husband had one child about my baby sister's age. Ada Marie was a lovely, lovely woman who died of cancer at thirty-five leaving an adoring husband and three wonderful bright, children.

Grandparents Frank and Ada also owned a farm. They grew fruits and vegetables that Grandpa would take to the Akron Farmers Market. Growing up, my brother and I spent a week or two every summer with these grandparents. My Aunt Helen and Uncle Dick had a fruit stand on the main road that went to Akron. People would stop on their way home from work or shopping at the grocery store in Copley. My brother and I often spent time sitting with our relatives at the fruit stand. It was fun to nibble on the berries. During strawberry season, Grandma would make shortcake. She would serve it warm with squashed fresh berries, topped with fresh whipped cream. Yummy, yummy, yummy! My grandparents always kept a cow or two for fresh milk. I would later make my shortcake with Bisquick and add vanilla ice cream. Now, sadly I am allergic to strawberries.

Grandma Ada's birthday was July 14th so the big family reunion was always the Sunday nearest to that date. Strawberry shortcake, pies, an assortment of cakes and all kinds of good food would grace the table. All of the relatives seemed to like to cook and were very good at it. Not as simple and plain as my other relatives, probably not as healthy with the butter and whipped cream. The kids would sometimes play yard games like softball, horseshoes or Red Rover. The younger adults would all take part in the fun or we would go play in the hay loft. We could have gotten hurt on the farm equipment, but never did. Sometimes, we were put to work picking up potatoes after an adult dug them up. Somehow, even work around these fun-loving relatives was always enjoyable. Even though I witnessed sibling rivalry I also saw the constant kidding and loving fun.

Now some families are having destination family reunions. With so many families scattered all over the country, sometimes a central location works better. Some people like to go to a beach location and rent a large house or several houses close by. Or a lake vacation could be fun with fishing and hiking and may not be as expensive. Check out www. homeaway.com – Okay? I'll take the beach, baby – or the mountains. I think family reunions are a neat way to stay in contact with your relatives. It has been years since I have been with any of my cousins. It seems, sometimes, weddings or funerals are the place to catch up, but definitely not as fun as a planned reunion. What do you think?

Things you can do to make your family reunions easier and more fun: If you have a large family, you may want to use www.familydetails.com and put a link on your invitations. This will help to keep the communication flowing and not drive you crazy. Keep the expenses reasonable. Figure out the shared meals ahead of time and ask for the shared expenses to be paid for in advance. Go for some simple fun activities like water balloon wars, plan a scavenger hunt or softball game. You might want to rent equipment for fun flicks or borrow a projector from a friend for movie night. You could rig up a white sheet as a movie screen.

Maybe you might want to ask your kin to bring family photos to share. Perhaps cover a large piece of cardboard with fabric and ribbon to insert photos for the family to guess who the people are or use smaller photo boards to pass around. Ask your relatives to bring extra copies to share.

Old photos of ancestors who have passed may be of interest, too.

You might want to include "family tee-shirts" as part of the reunion package. Another fun idea would be to put together a family history booklet to be given as a take-home memento. Check out www.styleunveiled.com's family tree. For a take-home memento, have everyone bring their favorite recipes on four-by-six cards. (Ask for as many copies as you have families.) Fix cute boxes with perhaps the family name on top.

Have the guests write a few paragraphs about their favorite past reunions, the time of reunion, place, who attended and what made it special. If you have them send on an eight-and-one-half-by-eleven sheet you could then make copies and give them out at the end of the reunion. Hopefully, with the right planning, you will have some wonderful memories to savor.

P.S. Everyone I know has had a few or at least one crazy relative. So, baby, don't think you are the only one, okay?

Chapter 22 *Fun With Hubby Not a Doberman*

Hubby is kind of like an old Doberman or maybe more like an old Dalmatian. A bit stubborn with a few old age spots. Definitely not show quality at his age. Maybe much younger he could have been considered borderline show. In retrospect, I would have done better with a husband like a Doberman Pinscher puppy. Why? Because the Dobies I've been around were sleek, had beautiful bodies and are considered to be highly trainable. (See where I'm going?) In the spring of 2014 I had a big problem with my sciatic nerve. It sent me to the chiropractor. A couple of days later "STUPID ASS ME" picked up a bag of books that maybe weighed twenty-five pounds. That gave me over-the-edge pain. I had Hubby get the walker out of the attic. (I had used it in recovering from knee replacement.) I should say, from "an old tennis injury." Not really, but it probably sounds better.

Hubby and I made the rounds. (FYI, Hubby will believe anything an M.D. tells him.) Me, not usually. He took me everywhere. I had to go to the acupuncturist, then chiropractor on different days. If you haven't had that opportunity – go for it. The ones I've gone to are very caring and professional, and usually they spend more time with clients than doctors. Finally, I went to Ms. Physician's assistant. She gave me a shot and a prescription for inflammatory pain – very strong, but not a controlled substance like codeine. I hate that fuzzy brain and constipation it brings on. This was the case when I had to be on that strong stuff when I had a knee replacement. Ugh, Ugh, Ugh!!!

Hubby was trying to be "the good guy," but getting more and more irritated by having to fix meals, tote, fetch and driving the old bitch around. Get the picture? Meanwhile, his wife is not in "a happy place" and needs help. She also hates, hates, hates to ask for help and is wanting her normal life back

NOW. (The first forty years of being married were easier.)

Think about it, if boys and men were as easy to train as a Doberman, life for us females would be simpler, wouldn't it? If you ask a Dobie to fetch, he does. If you ask a Dobie to sit and hush, he does. If you ask a Dobie to walk beside you, he does. Does he frown at you? No, no, no.

A Dobie wouldn't do that – or a Dalmatian either for that matter. Does a dog adore you? Yes, yes, yes! Does he want to be with you forever? Yes, yes, yes. Does he complain about the food you give him? No, no, no. Does he take control of the remote? No, no, no. Does he ask you to do the washing or ironing? NO! Does he like to watch the same TV shows as you? Yes, of course! Does he complain about the time you spend with your girlfriends? No, no, no!

Does he love to cuddle without – "expectations?" Yes! Does he have issues with you? No. Does he like your cooking even when it is leftovers? Yes, yes, yes! Does a well-trained Doberman leave a mess in the bathroom or bedroom? No. A well-trained man doesn't either. Mothers, train your sons! Hey, daughter-in law, I tried. I'm not sure where the slob genes come from – not his parents. Does he make you happy? Actually, I have to say Hubby is a neater, nicer person than I am. However, he has a lot of facial wrinkles from frowning at me. Yes, unfortunately at me and maybe our boys at times.

But why would a longtime breeder want a hubby like a Doberman instead of a Dalmatian? Dalmatians are the most adorable puppies. As they grow they become like a VERY BRIGHT four-year-old. Even if you are very intelligent, they can and often do outsmart you. But keep in mind, they were bred to keep up with a horse for eight hours. Think of the energy it would take.

No, lady, they aren't hyper, they are "athletic running machines" that need plenty of exercise EVERY DAY! They ARE stupid when it comes to cars. If they are hit they are gone. More than a few I have heard of have died that way. Years ago one of my Dals accidentally got out and, yes, got hit. Dals are also big-time mischief-makers, especially if they get bored. Would you leave a very bright four-year-old home alone and expect him not to get into anything? No.

A very cute Dalmatian bitch I sold years ago was exercised in the morning before her owner went to teach. She left her in her crate with fresh water. She also left the radio on to keep her company. Her laundry room was larger than most, with a window. My friend had purchased a large package of toilet paper. When she came home, her Dal was sitting in a large cloud of tiny pieces of toilet tissue she had pulled through her wire crate and torn up. How could my friend not laugh? I may have a jaded view but I don't think a Dobie would be that mischievous and maybe not as much fun. But what do I know?

I will say that most of the hundreds of Dalmatian people I've met are very bright and have a wonderful sense of humor. Mischievous, you bet. As you now know, Dals are an active fun breed. They are not for everyone. They are LOTS of fun but need a LOT of training and a chance to be active. (Playing ball, running in a yard or running on a lead next to you.) They need this every day and they need a strong master or mistress.

If Dal puppies weren't so sweet and cute we couldn't put up with them. Older Dals are a blessing, especially for an older person. Another plus is that they can move from one owner to another and be a loyal companion to the new owner within two or three days. I've had one returned at a year; another came to live with us at five. Both adjusted quickly and were not problems. So, if you get the opportunity to get an older one, I say go for it. My Hubby, even though his mother tried hard to train him, is not like a Doberman. He is more like an old Dalmatian, laidback and getting more spots. He is not fond of taking directions. Get my drift?

P.S. Honey, I still love you even though you aren't like a Doberman.

Chapter 23 *Fun At Garage Sales*

Years ago I met a thirteen-year-old and her mom at a garage sale in Roswell, Georgia. Today the young lady is college educated, married and the mother of two nearly school-aged girls. Her mom is counted as one of my "besties." Our relationship started with the daughter helping me with light housekeeping. When she got busy with soccer, mom asked if she could help me. She wanted a little extra spending money. Her husband, from South America, didn't want her working. She helped me and her husband never knew, as far as I know. Now we are friends who see each other about once a year. Would you believe a death at a garage sale? Actually, it happened at my last garage sale in Roswell. A young mother was turning left into our driveway. A fast-moving truck came over the small hill and didn't stop in time. The truck tires screeched and the truck hit the car on the driver's side. I think the baby in the back seat was killed instantly. The mother died soon afterward. When I heard the crash I dialed 911.

Jaws of Life were there soon but not soon enough to save the young teacher's entire family. How sad, sad, sad.

Fast-forward about twenty-five years, I tried again to have a garage sale in Florida. I decided after cleaning out our bonus room that I needed to get rid of A LOT of STUFF. I opened it up to our neighborhood. Three other families decided to do it too. I goofed, however, as I did not get it in our Wednesday local paper for Friday and Saturday. My neighbor was irritated with me so she changed it to Saturday and Sunday. I told everyone I would pay for the ad. The timing was way off – two weeks before Christmas. Another negative was when my neighbor got our community signs from storage. They said, "seven A.M. to one P.M." We had agreed our sale would be open eight-thirty A.M. to two-thirty P.M., which is what I put in the paper. I told my neighbor that the signs could easily be changed to nine to two. She said, "I'm not doing it." I said, "I'm still opening at eight-thirty A.M." She said, "You can do whatever you want; I am so over this as I am stressing out with my house on the market." (It had been on the market maybe two years.) I said, "I know how that is as our Roswell property was on the market for five years." (Due to zoning issues.) On Saturday we got really very good traffic. I felt it was a LOT of work and VERY tiring for very little money. My cottage furniture hardly got a look. Apparently people were looking for Christmas gifts. I had some interest in my beautiful queen-size sleeper. I declined an offer I should have taken for four hundred dollars.

Hubby made my day by saying, "You aren't going to have any more garage sales as long as I am alive." I almost always am a smart-ass. So I said, "Maybe I can hasten that a bit." (Bad girl that I am.) Hubby didn't bat an eye.

I have a lot more stuff that I don't want to give away. What to do? I decided to pack it up and take it to a friend's future garage sale. Some of the stuff I'll get a friend to post on Craig's List, some to consignment or perhaps I'll put an ad in the paper. I believe in giving and am going to give the majority of stuff to charity, but I need money to fund the redecorating of my leisure room. I know I can get a better price if I pay cash to my upholsterer for reupholstering work done.

The bottom line is that I still had my lovely sleeper in Hubby's garage. New, as it was a special order, it was normally twelve hundred dollars. I got it for twenty percent less on a special custom sale. It was made by Lazy Boy in a pricey, durable, and stylish floral with rolled arms. I just loved it. It had a very comfortable inner-spring mattress. It had been slept on three or four times and had been in my unused bonus room. After turning down four hundred dollars, I later had two women who wanted it but it was too big for their room, (Measure, people, measure.)

My Hubby got tired of having the covered sleeper in "his" garage. I told him the best way to sell it and all the other stuff was another garage sale. A few months later he agreed, IF I would get the rest of the stuff out of there in a week. A friend brought her stuff over and we agreed to do it together. The ad went in on Wednesday and Friday. The weather was pretty good but our traffic was really low. Too many other people were having community garage sales or charity garage sales. I made one hundred thirty dollars. My friend had a couple of high-ticket items so sold more. I had a guy who seemed interested in the sleeper. He wanted to bring his wife back to see it. I gave him our phone number. Hubby and I packed up a large load of stuff and took to our local charity. The guy did come by and his wife liked it. While I was in Ohio, my husband told me on the phone the guy offered three hundred dollars. I said I would call him when I got back. (I wasn't thrilled at the price.)

Three days after I got home he called again. I told him I had turned down four hundred dollars. He said, "Really?" I told him what I had paid and that I had taken very good care of it, etc. Then I said, "Would you go to three hundred fifty dollars?" He told me he had to pay someone to deliver it. I told him I had planned to put an ad in the paper to advertise the sofa and the cottage furniture, if he didn't want it. He agreed to pay three hundred and fifty dollars. I told him I needed cash. He said he understood. I knew he wanted it or he wouldn't have called back. I took a chance. If he had said he wasn't willing to go to three hundred fifty I would have had to "cave in" as Hubby was getting really irritated with me. I even had to give him the phone number of the nice guys I know who delivered furniture for a friend's furniture store. Sidebar: The movers told me the buyer complained about the sixty dollar delivery charge. They had to carry it a long way and pass two very pricey cars in the driveway. Oh well, (Love small towns).

My advice to you on garage sales: Plan yours for a Friday and Saturday. Plan ahead with your neighbors. Get people to agree on times and days. Do not plan to have your sale around the holidays. Hopefully, you will have it in good weather, but be prepared for rain or very cold weather. Maybe serve cold drinks in hot weather or coffee in cold. I had a small heater, but at thirty-four degrees it was still cold, cold, cold! Gloves helped. It is helpful to have a friend to help you, especially the first morning. You need someone as a "look-out." Several people have told me they have had things stolen when they either went to the bathroom or were looking the other way. Hopefully, you'll make money. A friend who always makes money told me to price items at about one-third of the cost (if in good condition) but know people will almost always want to pay less. Try not to be put off at anything anyone says. When buying at garage sales, try not to offend. When you want to pay less, try saying, "Would you consider a lower price?" Or you might say, "I really like this item, but I can only afford _____." Or, you can say, especially late on the last day of the sale, "What is your best price?" Often people will let things go for less if they like you.

Think before you buy. Ask yourself, "Do I need this item or is it just something I want?" Want is never need at any time. P.S. It probably isn't a good idea to buy a personal vibrator at a garage sale. Probably not the place to try to sell one, either... I'm just saying.

Chapter 24 *Fun Remembering*

When I was seventeen our family got a television set. (Question, why did they call it a "set" when there was only one?) It is hard for many of you to believe but our only station choices were NBC, CBS, and ABC and they were only in black and white. As someone said, "That is the way it was..." My favorite shows were "I Love Lucy," "The Tonight Show" and "The Jack Paar Show." I loved all the various comic hosts. Steve Allen was a comic genius. Yes, better than Johnny. I might add, that he took more risks on a lower budget. Steve was a multitalented person. I remember he published a funny edition of some children's stories. If I remember correctly, one was a bebop version of "Little Red Riding Hood." I also loved "The Ed Sullivan Show." I remember the first appearance of Elvis and also The Beatles. I always loved any of the comics and most of the theater shows. Most shows on TV at this time were ALL live, so anything could happen. I remember a young Carol Burnett on "The Gary Moore Show" and Johnny Carson on a variety show (probably as a guest comic on "The Tonight Show"). Then there was Joan River's first appearance on "The Tonight Show." Who could forget "American Bandstand"?

Early in our marriage Hubby and I would often watch TV together. We didn't have the money to go out. When we were first married we lived in Hartford, Connecticut. We both worked full time and would attend an occasional movie. Then we lived it up and went to see jazz legend Ella Fitzgerald. Our other entertainment consisted of dinner parties where I would make a simple meal with a nice dessert; often it was a German chocolate cake made from scratch. I used my cocoa 4-H Club icing. It was wonderful, kind of like me, ha ha (sweet on the outside and full of unnecessary calories inside).

For many people, social functions included food and TV. This still happens during big sports events, doesn't it? If I were doing this today I would get Sonny's Bar-B-Q – pulled pork, their beans and coleslaw and maybe a dessert – maybe. Lazy? Believe so.

One of the funniest skits on TV involved Jack Paar playing a husband. The couple had gone out for the evening and upon arriving back home, Jack says, "I'm going to catch the news." The very attractive wife says, "I'm going to bed." She kisses Jack. Next scene the wife is taking off her wig (during the sixties when we all tried to outdo our friends with the cutest wig). When the wife removes her wig she places it on a stool. She proceeds to take off her false eyelashes and places them on the wig. Following were her falsies and her girdle. You only see her arm placing the items on the stool. Next scene is her back view in a robe. The following scene is

Jack looking at all the stuff and waving a kiss towards the stool and saying, "Good night, love." This was a funny highlight of the week and maybe for the year for me. I just thought it was very clever.

FYI: Jack Paar had the Beatles on "The Tonight Show" before they were on the "Ed Sullivan Show." Frankly, I loved Jack Paar and Steve Allen on "The Tonight Show" better. I loved Johnny but I liked Jack and Steve better because I felt them to be more creative. I believe they both had less budget and longer, "live" shows. I seem to remember Jack and Steve having difficulties with the network executives. Sometimes talent is not always appreciated especially if they think or know what works for them or want more money. It seems to be common knowledge that Regis left his show, "Live With Regis and Kelly," due to money issues. He seemed to be crushed over the whole event. Regis told Dave Letterman that he missed being able to tell people about the interesting times he'd had with other celebrities and his life.

P.S. Bet it is not an easy time for Regis' wife, Joy. What do you do with that ego?

And then there are the old commercials like, "Plop, plop, fizz, fizz. Oh what a relief it is." Remember that? What about, "Tums for the tummy"? Remembering these MAY mean you are no longer young. "Things go better with Coke, It's the real thing. I'd like to buy the world a Coke and Coke adds life." Or, from their chief competition, "Come alive, you're in the Pepsi generation, "or "Feeling free! Take the Pepsi challenge!" Pepsi got a real shot of popularity after the famous old movie star, Barbara Stanwick, married the CEO. She then became the CEO after her husband died. I guess that proved she was more than "just attractive."

Remember "I've fallen and I can't get up?" I've been there, unfortunately. Or how about Ginsu knives? "It slices, it dices!" Did I hear that bad girl, Lorena Bobbitt, works for them now? Remember in a fit of passion she chopped off her husband's you-know-what? I also heard he went to work for Snap-On Tools. Is that right? Or wrong? Or just funny??? I thought it very creative and funny.

There used to be a LOT of cigarette ads. Remember "I'd walk a mile for a Camel?" Not me, baby! It is a nasty, smelly cancer-producing habit. Having lost two very close friends to lung cancer I have very strong feelings about smoking. It is hard to believe that the following actually ran on TV. One of the ads said, "Just what the doctor ordered." SICK. Then, "Winston tastes good like a cigarette should," "You've come a long way, baby" and "I'd rather fight than switch." But what about, "More doctors smoke Camels than any other cigarette!" Yes, lots of doctors in the forties, fifties, sixties, seventies and, yes, the eighties did smoke.

A favorite old commercial is the Oscar Mayer wiener. "Oh, I wish I were an Oscar Mayer Wiener. That is what I truly would like to be. Cause if I were an Oscar Mayer Wiener, everyone would be in love with me!" Maybe your old favorite was Brylcreem. "A little dab'll do ya!" There was, "Ding dong, Avon calling" and "Kind of young, kind of now..." from a Charlie (perfume) ad. For years I used Ivory soap. (What happened to it?) "Ninety-nine and forty-four percent pure." Pure what? Hey, girlfriends, remember the Aqua Velva man? The commercial was, "There's something about an Aqua Velva man." Man, was there. Another grooming ad was, "Does she...or doesn't she?" by Clairol. Until now only my Hubby, kids and hairdresser knew what I used.

The Milk Bone ads used, "Cleans teeth, freshens breath, naturally." Not always, but the human food commercials went on and on. "It takes two hands to handle a Whopper." Do you remember the old lady saying, "Where's the beef?" "Have it your way" at Burger King. "Kiss my grits" wasn't about food, but was in a saying in a popular television show. Lots of "jeans ads" in the old days were for Jordache, Calvins, Chic and Gloria Vanderbilt. Gloria was a real hottie in the fifties and sixties. She still has her "jean line" but may be better known as Anderson Cooper's mother. They wrote a best-selling book "The Rainbow Comes And Goes." I thought the book interesting reading.

"Mm! Mm! good, Mm! Mm! good. That's what Campbell's soup is." "I am stuck on Band-Aids 'cause Band-Aids stuck on me." Ha ha. For the mentally challenged, "Sometimes you feel like a nut. Sometimes you don't." For a refreshing idea, "Put a Tic Tac in your mouth and get a bang out of life." Isn't that something? It takes more than a couple of Tic Tics for me to get a bang. Am I slow or old? Probably both. Miss some of those commercials, but don't these ads bring back memories of the simpler times?

P.S. Pop, pop, there goes my energy drink. I love V-8 VFusion diet energy drink. It contains: water, reconstituted vegetable juice blend (water and concentrated juices of sweet potatoes, purple carrots, reconstituted fruit blend (water and concentrated juices of apples, white grapes, cranberries, red raspberries), contains less than 2% of citric acid, malic acid, natural flavors, raspberry juice concentrate, green tea extract (with natural caffeine from green tea), vitamin C, sucralose, niacin amide (vitamin B3), vitamin B2 and vitamin B12. It is sweetened with a nonnutritive sweetener. The ad on the can says it burns calories plus has lasting energy and is clinically proven. Sure, that's why I'm so slender, right? If that is so, why do I still have a fat ass?

Fun With Reality Shows

Can you turn them off once you see what might or might not happen? Oh my, oh my, how could I waste years watching some of my favorites? Maybe that is why it has taken me awhile to write book two and three. I do have to admit that I often write while watching television.

Guess what? I'm watching "The Millionaire Match Maker." Then I switch to "Kourtney and Kim Take Miami." I think I have seen both of these shows before. I can't believe I would watch that "stuff" twice.

While standing in line at the grocery store I picked up a shiny magazine because it had a photo and story about the latest Bachelor. I started talking to the guy behind me. (By this time you know I'll talk to anyone.) I said, "You don't have to watch 'The Bachelor' if you pick up a magazine and read all about him." The man told me his daughter was on "that show" several years ago. He told me the entire show is scripted. "No," I said, "but I'm not surprised as I figured that most of all the reality shows are scripted." He told me that his daughter played the "kind of crazy" girl. Then he told me that they wanted her to be the "new" bachelorette. (She had done the show to help her modeling resume.) He went on to tell me that his daughter was engaged before she did the show. She told the network that they couldn't pay her enough to do another show. She married her fiancé, a CEO who got transferred from Jacksonville, Florida, to New York City. I wished I could have asked him how much they gave her to put her life on hold for however long it took to shoot the show.   Recently I met someone who had a cousin in Alaska who was on HGTV. I believe it was the house-hunting show. This gal told me her cousin had their home for six months before being on the show. So much for reality!

I recently met a gal who was on "Family Feud." She told me they didn't make it to the next level. She said it was fun. When I asked if they were paid, she said no.

P.S. Lesson here is don't believe all you see or hear – reality isn't real.

Chapter 25 *Fun Traveling To Tulsa*

In the spring of 2012, I headed to Tulsa, Oklahoma, to the Dalmatian Club of America's Specialty (an annual show). Dalmatian events go on for nearly a week. These include obedience trials, road trails where the dogs keep up with their owner on a horse, agility trials and conformation classes. Conformation shows are what you have seen on television, from New York at Madison Square Garden, etc. The dogs are judged on the standard of each breed, how their body parts are aligned, their condition, movement, spotting, grooming and personality. It is called a "dog show" so they need to wag their tails.

I don't go into the ring and show Dals anymore but I do co-own dogs that are being shown. I think it is always more fun to show your own dogs. However, I still enjoy going to shows to see our dogs and to hang out with my "fun doggie friends." My Florida co-owners, Cheryl and Buddy, drove from Tampa to Tulsa, while I flew. Due to hotel and travel expenses we decided to skip several days, arriving in time for our spotted darling girls to show. We found out that an "intestinal bug" was affecting many of the humans. We tried to be careful using wipes, washing our hands frequently, etc. In spite of our efforts, on the last day Buddy and I both got ill. Buddy vomited.

I just felt miserable, having horrible stomach pains. I thought I had forgotten to take my Zantac, which my doctor prescribed several years ago. I think Buddy got to feeling better as he got it out of his system faster. I felt bad for a couple of days. Not feeling well meant that it was difficult to function properly. I managed to pack up and get on my flight to Dallas, Texas, where I had a two-hour layover, before heading back to Florida.

The layover is where I got in trouble – big time. How can a person miss their flight if they are at the airport three hours before flight time? Remember, I did this in Atlanta on my trip to Europe to meet my grandson. I swore to myself I wouldn't do it again. This may be hard to believe but not feeling well I went into a restaurant/bar to get a glass of ginger ale. I thought I would also get toast or a baked potato to help settle my stomach. Turns out they didn't have any of the above. The waiter talked me into having a glass of Chardonnay. He said it should help settle my stomach. It had been hours since I had toast and a Coke.

I got to talking to some forty-year-olds. Three gals and a guy, none traveling together. Next thing I know the guy insists on buying me more wine. I had a ball with them. They all bought a book of mine. The guy had to go to an ATM to get money to do so, very funny. I was feeling no pain. Suddenly I realized I needed to head to my gate and found out I had just missed my plane.

The American Airlines person said they would probably be able to get me on the next and last flight of the day, five hours later. Oh well, I love to people watch and talk to people. The last plane was loading and it still looked like I might get on until the very last minute. By this time it was about eight P.M. I wasn't able to get on. An American agent was so lovely she helped me get a hotel. I thought I had lost my cell phone. Turns out I found I had packed it the side pocket of my carry on the night before and didn't find it for several days. Someone let me use their cell phone to call my husband. He was very understanding as I told him I missed my flight because I wasn't feeling well. (Well, I hadn't been.)

I got to the hotel – thank God for credit cards. I did have cash for the tips. I paid the limo driver. When I got to the hotel I had to take advantage of the free toothbrush, etc. All I had with me was a few books and a black knit, long sundress I had worn to a banquet with a jacket. I had packed it around my books to keep them from moving around. I had the books with me to sell at the airport. Several ladies going to Hawaii were thrilled to have something fun to read. I sold about ten, yeah!

I had to get up at 4:30 A.M. to catch my plane. Since I can never seem to get to sleep before midnight, it was a short night. Arriving home, it took several days to unpack and find my cell, then get it reconnected. Hey folks, I had had an interesting and for the most part a fun adventure.

P.S. Isn't my life full of surprises? Aren't you somewhat jealous of all my fun??? Yeah, sure.

Chapter 26 *Fun Living Better For Less*

According to author Ernest Callenbach who wrote *Living Cheaply With Style*, you can live better spending less. He claims that by buying a good quality used car you gain more down the road than buying a less expensive new car. An upgraded used car will cost a lot less than a new one and probably last longer. Ask for service records and have a trusted mechanic check it out.

Mr. Callenbach suggests you de-clutter your home. Maybe you need to have a garage sale. (A good idea is to plan one with your neighbors so you can share the advertising and attract more people). My designer friend, Randy, suggests you advertise on Craig's List.

Callenbach says, "Instead of just spending less, you may actually make money if you sell your stuff..." He also says, "The more stuff you own, the more time, energy and money you spend to maintain it." Clearing your home of clutter will help you have less stress and confusion in your life.
(Note to self – do this, Emily.) Next time you are thinking of celebrating, go out for lunch instead of having dinner. The portions are smaller as is the expense. Spending time with your friends and or loved ones makes any get-together a fun time and one to remember.

Think about paying cash for most of your purchases. It makes you stop and think before over-spending. Keep a small notebook in your bag and write down every purchase, including your cola or coffee. Be aware. A credit card is not always a good idea.

Fun Money-Saving Tips from my Typist, Leslie

There are so many ways to live "on a budget," but I was lucky enough to come up with a great plan to help me make the monthly bills and have a little money for personal shopping. In a day that most people are warned about using credit cards, I have found a plan using my credit cards as well as my checkbook. Old-fashioned, yes, but it works for me. I do have all my regular bills broken down into twelve months a year, and use those figures to form my monthly budget. I have a monthly graph in the registry of my checkbook to keep track of every purchase I make. If there is money left over in one of the categories at the end of the month it is carried over to the next month. This helps me save up for expensive bills, such as medical, auto insurance or repairs. When something is purchased with a credit card, I record it as being spent (I put a small mark next to it in my checkbook to remind me it is a credit card purchase) until the bill comes. That way in my mind it is spent and therefore keeps me accountable for my spending. Best of all when the bill comes in at the end of the month the money is there for it to be paid.

Credit Cards

We often hear how bad careless use of credit cards can be. I use them for most of my purchases. I have three cards. One of them pays rewards for gasoline purchases. Gas is the only thing I use it for and every month when the bill comes, I get a small rebate that gives me a credit toward the money I owe. It's usually not much, but every little bit helps. The key for me is to ALWAYS pay the entire balance off every month. I'm not sure if there are many cards out there anymore that give points, but I have a Visa card from a well-known clothing company. I buy some things from the store when it is a VERY good sale, which gives me double rebate points, then also for most of my other monthly purchases, which gives me a smaller amount of points. I allow these points to add up and use them to buy some very nice Christmas gifts and occasionally a new piece for my wardrobe for free. Unfortunately, the store closed so I no longer get my super clothing savings. My other clothing secrets are garage sales, local consignment and thrift shops. I look for good brand items and sometimes even find new things with the new tags still on them. When I buy out of season to wear for the following year, however, I have to make sure to remember I have them in the back of my closet or packed under my bed.

Ultimate Coupons

Who has not seen or heard of the television show, "Ultimate Couponing"? It seems to be "all the rage" for people willing to work hard to make the "ultimate savings" on their groceries. Stores seem to have a pricing system that includes distributing coupons and later offering those items for a sale price. If you take the time to learn what goes on sale and when, then collect coupons to use toward your sale purchase, you can save a significant amount of money at the store.

Housing

Rent is a very hard expense for many. I myself "barter" for my room and board. I am caregiver and chauffeur for an elderly relative in exchange for a room and food. I was told about an idea I have never heard of. Some people house-sit for long periods of time while homeowners are out of town. Recently, I heard of house-sitting in a home that was "staged" and was up for sale. That allows you to live in a home that is for sale in exchange for keeping it clean and tidy and ready to be shown to potential buyers at any given time. It is my understanding that utility bills (and of course your food) would be your only living expenses. The friend that told me about this said she even knew of a couple that were allowed to use their own very nice furniture to stage the house. Having roommates is another way to save money. Make sure you have everything in writing. It could be a real nightmare if they aren't responsible and you are the one who signed the lease.

Sidebar: I met someone who rents a very nice three-bedroom home in a high-rent area. Normal rent would be up to two thousand dollars a month but this couple only pays five hundred dollars a month, plus utilities. They got this really good deal because the house is for sale. They are there to stage it with their own furniture, keep it clean and have it available for showings. If you are a really neat person it might not be so bad. I would have to be desperate to do that as I am not a neat person.

Obviously I have kept our houses neat when they were for sale but it sure wasn't easy, baby. Actually I have known three couples who have done this; two of the couples finally bought their own home.

I am sure there are many other ways to cut corners when it comes to living in today's world. There is everything from clipping coupons to using rebate sites on the internet. The bottom line is finding the right plan for you.

Discounts for Those Fifty and Over

Restaurants

Applebee's: fifteen percent off with a Golden Apple Card (60 plus)

Arby's: ten percent off (55 plus)

Ben & Jerry's: ten percent off (60 plus)

Bennigan's: Discounts vary by location.

Bob's Big Boy: Discount varies by location (60 plus). Boston Market: ten percent off (65 plus)

Burger King: sixty percent off (60 plus)

Chick-Fil-A: ten percent off or free small drink or coffee (60 plus)

CiCi's Pizza: ten percent off (60 plus)

Denny's: ten percent off; twenty percent off for AARP members (55 plus)

Dunkin' Donuts: ten percent off (60 plus)

Einstein's Bagels: ten percent off baker's dozen (60 plus)

Gatti's Pizza: ten percent (60 plus)

Golden Corral: ten percent off (60 plus)

Hardee's: $0.33 beverages every day (65 plus)

IHOP: ten percent off (55 plus)

Jack in the Box: up to twenty percent off (55 plus) KFC: free small drink with any meal (55 plus)

Krispy Kreme: ten percent off (50 plus)
Long John Silver's: various discounts at locations (55 plus)

McDonald's: discounts on coffee every day (55 plus)

Mrs. Field's: ten percent off at participating locations (60 plus)

Shoney's: ten percent off

Sonic: ten percent off or free beverage (60 plus)

Steak and Shake ten percent off every Monday and Tuesday (50 plus)

Subway: ten percent off (60 plus)

Sweet Tomatoes: ten percent off (62 plus)

Taco Bell: five percent; free beverages for seniors (65 plus)

TCBY: ten percent off (55 plus)

Tea Room Café: ten percent off (50 plus)

Village Inn: ten percent off (60 plus)

Waffle House: ten percent off every Monday (60 plus)

Wendy's: ten percent off (55 plus)

Whataburger: ten percent off (62 plus)

White Castle: ten percent off (62 plus) – This is for me... If I ever see one again.

Retail & Apparel:

Banana Republic: thirty percent off (50 plus)

Beall's: twenty-five percent first Tuesday of each month (50 plus)

Belk's: fifteen percent off first Thursday of each month (50 plus)

Bon-Ton Department Stores: fifteen percent off on senior discount days (55 plus)

C.J. Banks: ten percent off every Wednesday (60 plus)

Clark's: ten percent off (62 plus)

Dress Barn: twenty percent off (55 plus)

Goodwill: ten percent off one day a week (dates vary by location)

Hallmark: ten percent off one day per week (date varies by location)

Kohl's: fifteen percent off (60 plus)

Modell's Sporting Goods: thirty percent off

Rite Aid: ten percent off on Tuesdays and ten percent off prescriptions

Ross Stores: ten percent off every Tuesday (55 plus)

The Salvation Army Thrift Stores: up to fifty percent off (55 plus)

Stein Mart: twenty percent off red dot/ clearance items first Monday of every month (55 plus)

T.J. Max: ten percent off on Tuesdays (varies by location)

Grocery

Albertson's: ten percent off first Wednesday of each month (55 plus)

American Discount Stores: ten percent off every Monday (55 plus)

Compare Foods Supermarket: ten percent off every Wednesday (60 plus)

DeCicco Family Markets: five percent off every Wednesday (60 plus)

Fry's Supermarket: free Fry's VIP Club Membership and ten percent off every Monday (55 plus)

Great Value Food Store: five percent off every Tuesday (60 plus)

Gristedes Supermarket: ten percent off every Tuesday (60 plus)

Harris Teeter: five percent off every Thursday (60 plus)

Hy-Vee: five percent off one day a week (date varies by location.)

Kroger: ten percent off (date varies by location)

Morton Williams Supermarkets: five percent off every Tuesday (60 plus)

The Plant Shed: ten percent off every Tuesday (50 plus)

Publix: Five percent off every Wednesday (55 plus)

Rogers Marketplace: five percent off every Thursday (60 plus)

Uncle Giuseppe's Marketplace: fifteen percent off (62 plus)

Travel

Alaska Airlines: fifty percent off (65 plus)

Continental Airlines: no initial fee for Continental President's Club and special fares for select destinations

Southwest Airlines: various discounts for ages 65 plus (call before booking)

Greyhound: fifteen percent off (62 plus)

Trailways Transportation System: various discounts for ages 65 plus

Alamo Car Rental: up to twenty-five percent off for AARP members

Avis: up to twenty-five percent off for AARP members

Budget Rental Cars: forty percent off; up to fifty percent off for AARP members

Dollar Rent-A-Car: ten percent off (50 plus)

Enterprise Rent-A-Car: five percent off for AARP members

Hertz: up to twenty-five percent for AARP members

National-Rent-A-Car: up to thirty percent off for AARP members

Overnight Accommodations

Holiday Inn: twenty to forty percent off depending on location (62 plus)

Best Western: forty percent off (55 plus)

Econo Lodge: forty-nine percent off (60 plus)

Hampton Inn & Suites: forty percent off when booked 72 hours in advance

Hyatt Hotels: twenty-five percent to fifty percent off (62 plus)

Intercontinental Hotel Groups: various discounts at all hotels (65 plus)

Marriott Hotels: twenty-five percent off (62 plus)

Motel 6: stay free Sunday nights (60 plus)

Myrtle Beach Resort: thirty percent off (55 plus)

Activities and Entertainment

(From www.free4seniors.com)

AMC Theaters: up to thirty percent off (50 plus)

Carmike Cinemas: thirty-five percent off (65 plus)

Busch Gardens, Tampa, Florida: $3.00 off one-day ticket (50 plus)

U.S. National Parks: $80.00 lifetime pass; fifty percent off additional services including camping (62) Regal Cinemas: Senior ticket (60 plus)

Ripley's Believe It Or Not: $2.00 off one-day pass (55 plus)

Sea World, Orlando, Florida: $3.00 off one-day ticket (50 plus)

Verizon Wireless: Verizon National 65 Plus Plan (65 plus)

Miscellaneous

Great Clips: $2.00 off haircuts (60 plus)

Supercuts: $2.00 off haircuts (60 plus)

The discounts on this list are listed on the website "The Senior List" found at www.theseniorlist.com.

Now, go out there and claim your discounts... and remember... You must ASK for the discount... no ask, no discount.

I know everyone knows someone over fifty, please pass the word on!!!

Chapter 27 *Fun In My Life*

I was not happy to leave my twenties – nor my thirties. I loved my twenties.

A lot happened during my twenties. I got pinned, graduated from college, got my first real job, got engaged, married and had two sons.

When I turned thirty in California I was teaching high school, kept our townhouse up, took care of Hubby and two sons, three and six. I was also going to graduate school one night a week. I also took a class I dearly loved on the history of jazz, from the University Of California. During the summers I drove back and forth to San Francisco State, taking classes.

We had moved into what became my favorite house in Los Altos, California. It was a white ranch board-and-batten with black shutters and front door. It was located at 14 Avalon Drive. We paid, I believe, $37,000. We loved that the garage was on the side of the house (facing Edith Ave.). Hubby and I worked hard on this thirteen-year-old house making it our home. Briefly, we washed walls, ceiling (four times as previous owner was a smoker), put up some wall paper etc. (More about these home projects in my almost completed next book, *Decorating Isn't A Joke Or Is It*). Three years later we sold it for $42,000. We didn't make any money after realtor fees and other expenses. We had a wonderful life there. We left to go to Atlanta for a new job opportunity for Hubby.

We lived in Tucker, Georgia, for three years before moving to just outside Roswell to have room for our Dalmatians. We had purchased our first show dog shortly before leaving California. Our home in Tucker had been new.

We had it sold quickly three years later, maybe making two thousand dollars.

The Roswell house needed constant repairs and remained our main residence for almost forty years. We lived in Tucker and bought a much more expensive property (eight acres plus our old house). I got too carried away with too many Dalmatians. (They are like chocolate chip cookies – one or two is often not enough.) The house was too large with too many projects for me to manage. Add to that, a lot of stress due to job problems and being a mom. We were not prepared for the furnace going out, plus the ceiling falling down, etc. We had some really fun parties at our home. We had some good family fun as well as some difficult times – as most families. During this time, one thing that was difficult for me was turning forty! I remember telling a friend I was having a big birthday. She said, "Forty?" I said, "No, fifty, that's why it hurt me when you said Hubby looked like one of my sons." That shut her up.

As I remember my forties were spent dealing with migraine headaches. A day without one was to be celebrated. I now feel that living in the dust of an old house plus lots of food, tree, grass, mold and weather-related allergies were to blame. (I took allergy shots for forty-two years.) In my fifties I remember lots of female problems with a hysterectomy and the removal of an eight-pound grade I cancerous tumor. About this time I had been teaching decorating and design classes for the Atlanta School of Art and Interior Design. When the school closed I opened my shop, "The Strawberry Unicorn" – decorating, antiques and art. I had taken a class on having a business. Unfortunately, I was unfinanced and not in the best location. The fact that I felt tired and yucky all the time didn't help. While going through the cancer surgery (no after-treatment was suggested) Hubby looked for a job in Florida.

However, the change would not have been good for our retirement. He suggested we get a small place north of Clearwater so I could get out of the not-good-for-me Atlanta climate. We spent as much time together as we could. Primarily my two or three Dals and I went back and forth. During this time I had a few more litters of puppies. I had some wonderful buyers, several that I still keep in touch with.

Unfortunately, I got the flu and was drinking too many diet colas and taking Excedrin day and night along with antibiotics. Soon I was very ill. I should have known when I lost my appetite. My youngest son and one of my puppy owners both called Hubby and told him he ought to get down there and check on me. I ended up in Morton Plant Hospital (in Clearwater) for three weeks with kidney failure. The doctor told me that in two more days I would have been dead. I was pretty much out of it for about ten days. I didn't give a damn about anything. It is a painless way to die. It was really hard to get my strength back. I went home with one son taking care of me for a week, the other one the next week. Hubby had to get back to work. Then I was on my own with three dogs – NOT easy. I was in a wheelchair whenever I went out for about ten days. I did chair exercises along with my PBS instructor. My local girlfriends were very supportive. Soon I was out doing stand-up. Then dropped "the Bomb" – we had to sell the Florida house due to the huge hospital bills.
(We had insurance but still had a huge co-pay.)

Back to Roswell with Hubby. I would escape to Florida when the weather was ugly, staying with friends or to go to a dog show. Hubby and I took several short trips to coastal Alabama and to the Florida First Coast looking for a future retirement location.

We put our Roswell place on the market. It was a difficult place to sell as the house sat seventy feet from a two-lane road which was in the process of becoming a six-lane. We were having a hard time getting it zoned commercial. We had it sold in a year, but unfortunately, they cancelled the DAY of closing. This time our Florida home was being built. But Hubby decided he wasn't ready to retire yet. I told him his company should give him a larger office with a bed, microwave and a bathroom. Ho ho.

Finally we sold our Roswell home and bought a townhouse a mile from Hubby's job. I went back and forth from Florida to Atlanta until we bought our North Carolina home. At that time we spent summers in North Carolina, three hours north of Atlanta, and winters in Florida.

Chapter 28 *Fun Remembering TV*

Aaron Spelling produced lots of television hits. Who doesn't remember Pacific Palisades, Malibu Shores, Sunset Beach or Seventh Heaven? Some of my younger friends really loved Melrose Place, Dynasty, Charlie's Angels and Hart to Hart. The Dick Powell Show was a favorite of mine. In addition, Tori Spelling's dad produced the following: The Embraced, after Jimmy Kindred, A Season in Purgatory, Models, Inc.; Robin Hoods, Burke's Law, University Hospital and Love on the Run, How about Jailbirds, The Heights and Grassroots, A Valentine Voyage, Beverly Hills 90210, Nightingales, Rich Men, Single Women, Cracking Up, Day One, International Airport, Hotel, Finders of Lost Loves, At Ease, T.J. Hooker, Strike Force, Making of a Male Model, Little Ladies of the Night and Maserati and the Brain? Who doesn't remember Fantasy Island or Starsky and Hutch?

Spelling had fun producing other television shows such as One of My Wives Is Missing, Cruise into Terror, Cry Panic and Death Sentence. Aaron also produced The Girl with Something Special (a favorite of our family), The Affair, The Bait Car, The Pigeon Street, The Bounty Man, The Chill Factor, The Rookies, Honey West and Johnny Ringo.

Spelling's TV movies were: The Ballad of Andy Crocker, Death Sentence, Snatched, Carter's Army, The Daughters of Joshua Cabe, The House that Would Not Die, Cry Panic, Death Cruise, In Broad Daylight, Five Desperate Women, and The Last Child. Wow, how did he have time to have two children??? If he hadn't been a pipe-smoker maybe he would have lived to produce lots more hits.

In the sixties, I loved The New Loretta Young Show. She was still beautiful even in older years. Maybe a facelift? What a lovely figure and she seemed to have been a lovely soul, too. Carol Burnett was on The Garry Moore Show and I fell in love with both of them. Our family enjoyed and watched many of the Gunsmoke and Bob Newhart shows. Variety shows with music and comedy were always fun to watch with the boys. We especially enjoyed The Danny Kaye Show, The Sid Caesar Show, The Steve Lawrence Show, The Carol Burnett Show, and the beautiful Phyllis Diller Show, Sing Along With Mitch, The Jack Paar Program and The Jonathan Winters Show. Some of these were on late so the boys didn't get to watch.

The seventies brought Jimmy Durante Presents, The Lennon Sisters Hour, The New Bill Cosby Show, The Julie Andrews Hour, and The Andy Williams Show.

During the sixties and seventies Hubby and I would sometimes watch shows such as Armstrong Circle Theater, The US Steel Hour, The DuPont Show of The Week, Alcoa

Premiere, Voice of Firestone, Alfred Hitchcock, CBS Reports, Sixty Minutes, Kojak and The Streets of San Francisco.

The mid-seventies and into the eighties, as a family we would watch The New Cosby Show, Charlie's Angels and Lou Grant. I would watch The Redd Foxx Comedy Hour or Falcon Crest. Who besides me wasn't in love with the adorable actor who played Remington Steele? Hotel, Miami Vice, Spencer: For Hire and L.A. Law were also interesting to watch. Also, girls, we can still see Designing Women, can't we? And oh how I loved Tracey Ullman. I don't think most of the TV shows today will be as fondly remembered as those in "the good old days."

What about the cigarette ads? Can you believe "More doctors smoke Camels than any other cigarette?" Hard to believe. Speaking of doctors, "I'm not a doctor but I play one on TV."

And think about, "Please don't squeeze the Charmin!" or, "Leggo of my Eggo!"

Did you love Upstairs, Downstairs as much as I did? Oh and how can we forget The Galloping Gourmet or the cooking shows on PBS?

Our sons loved Wagon Train, Gunsmoke and Death Valley Days after they outgrew Captain Kangaroo, Howdy Doody and Shari Lewis and Lambchop.
(Truth be told, I probably liked Shari's shows more than the boys.

What a success M.A.S.H. was and apparently still is. As I notice it when I am surfing the TV. Many of my friends and I would comment on the interactions and relationships, for instance, the married couples on Married with Children, Laverne and Shirley, All In the Family, The Jefferson's, and The Flintstones (one of the cutest cartoon shows ever).

In the beginning   before color TV, we loved The Honeymooners and I Love Lucy, didn't we? They and Sid Caesar set the comic tone for others to come – such as Archie Bunker and George Jefferson, etc.

Do any of you remember the outer space shows such as Lost in Space and Buck Rogers in the 25th Century? I do recall the boys teasing each other about hoping the other would get lost in space. Let's not forget the black-and-white Lassie show and Chuck Wagon dog food ads. Then there was Flipper and The Undersea World of Jacques Cousteau. What young guy could resist Baywatch or Sea Hunt?

We can't let this subject go without mentioning The Facts of Life, Small Wonder, My Two Dads, Full House and Punky Brewster. Oh, I nearly forgot, "the game shows." Let's Make a Deal, Truth or Consequences, Match Game and Kathie Lee on Name That Tune. She has had an amazing life and longevity, much as Barbara Walters. Of course, Password, Jeopardy, High Rollers and The Price is Right should not be forgotten either.

Is there anyone over thirty that doesn't remember Dick Clark? He was such a handsome charming host on American Bandstand, wasn't he? Had I been him, I would have wanted to retire from TV before saliva was dripping from my mouth and few could understand me.

P.S. Do hope you older people enjoy the memories that are associated with these TV shows and commercials. I know I love looking back but know in my heart that we need to live in the moment and plan for good things (with God's help) in the future.

Chapter 29 *Fun Getting Older, Maybe*

You lie down for a nap and someone thinks you're dead. No one tells you – slow down, you'll break your neck. They don't have to. After several falls, eventually you'll have to have your knee replaced. Could your ass be next?

You know guys who have eyebrows that look like shrubs and nose hair long enough to be fish bait. You worry that someday the eyebrow hair will join the nasal hair and you won't be able to see their faces. Maybe that wouldn't be so bad. You know God has a weird sense of humor, don't you? Otherwise, your legs wouldn't look like road maps and you wouldn't have to shave your chin daily.

When you were young you may have had an "achy breaky heart." Now as you get older you know more people who have had various heart surgeries. We all get jealous when someone dies of a heart attack. Why? It beats dying slowly in pain. Years ago you didn't know what a colonoscopy was; now you have one on a regular basis. At least you get a lot of sympathy for the pre-treatment. Oh, those lovely drinks you have to drink. What about being "up all night"? The actual procedure isn't all that bad. Afterwards, at your next meal, you can pig out and not gain weight. Yeah!

You know you are getting older when your racing mind is on fast forward and your body seems to be in reverse or maybe you are having "brain farts"??? You're thinking, "If I knew I was going to live this long I know I would have taken better care of myself." (Who originally said this, I don't know.) Taking care of yourself requires a lot of effort, namely exercise, diet and regular checkups. Now anyone over twenty pounds overweight is considered obese. I qualify, darn it, at twenty-two to twenty-five pounds over. I would go to a group In North Carolina where I weighed in every week; otherwise I would have been fighting even more pounds. I try to get on my exercise machine and walk upstairs every day. (Notice I said try.) I also go to an hour of chair yoga weekly.

Sometimes getting older is a real pain in the ass – literally. Sciatic pain in the hip joint came on after a couple of long trips. It is NOT fun! It is almost constant sharp pain – walking, sitting, standing and lying down. (That, cookie, is one of the reasons old people can be grumpy.) I went to outpatient therapy for several months to get rid of the pain. In Florida the therapist had me do different exercises with a rub-down at the end. This was done through my clothes. When I went to North Carolina for the summer I had to stop every hour and a half and do some exercises. I also put a pillow under my butt so I was sitting higher at the spine which helped a lot. In Florida the therapy was with the same person every time; however, in North Carolina I had a team. Maybe the very tall, handsome therapist/owner was a former baseball pitcher for the Dunedin Blue Jays. I'm guessing, but I would think the blue-eyed hunk was probably in his late thirties and has a cute personality. This North Carolina therapist had me lie on the massage table face down. Then behind draperies pulls down my panties a little to do a deep massage on my sore hip. I said, bad gal that I am, "It has been a long time since I have had a guy pull my panties down." He laughed. Fall of 2016 I called and made an appointment to go in after back surgery. There he was, blue eyes grinning at seeing me. I had not seen him the previous summer. I said, "Hi, remember me?" "Yes," he said as he blushed, bless his heart.

As I write this, I am thinking more and more about getting into a regular exercise program – ugh, ugh, UGH! From

115

age thirty my weight has been a challenge. I used to keep active and loved showing my dogs. This sport helped me keep my weight down. I showed the Dalmatians myself until I was about sixty.

I went to Curves for about ten years until they closed. I used to complain a lot about going to Curves; however, I really benefited. You know that saying, "If you don't use it, you lose it." I felt better, looked better and had more energy when I exercised three times a week. Exercising at home hasn't been doing it for me; I am a lazy person. I need to find a gym. Can't say I am looking forward to that. I do not want cancer (again) or heart problems. I can tell you that lots of older people I have known have had major health problems probably as a result of being overweight and out of shape.

Long story short, it isn't easy getting older. You can have fun but it requires getting out, being active and getting involved in church or community activities. It also requires keeping doctor visits so that little problems don't become big ones. You need to keep a positive attitude and surround yourself with happy people, who add fun to your life.

Bring on the music, food, wine and fun! And handsome topless male dancers might add to the fun!

Chapter 30 Fun Changing Your Man

I have been reading parts of *A Woman's Guide To Changing Her Man* by Michelle Weiner-Davis. She seems to think that by changing your actions you can change your man. I'm wondering if I can change the man I have been married to for over fifty years??? He would tell you he doesn't need changing. Yeah, sure ~ and the world is flat, right?

How would I like him to change? Although, I am blessed to be married to a sweet, caring good person, he can drive me a little crazy at times. For instance, if I'm at home he NEVER makes any attempt to answer the phone. NONE. If I'm not home he usually answers if he hears it. He doesn't always write down who it is and he gets my girlfriends mixed up. Maybe he could ask my girlfriends how they spell their names, then write me a note with their phone number. Since I am a realist I don't see that happening. I have taught old dogs new tricks, but an old husband, not yet.

Okay, I'm thinking of a couple more changes that would be nice. Would it be possible to get him to stop frowning at most everything I say? Could he say things like, "Honey, could we watch a chick movie on television tonight?" or what about, "Sweetheart, I'll make a salad, bake us a couple of sweet potatoes and grill us a couple of steaks, okay???" Or what about, "Honey, I have a whole day to go shopping with you. Where do you want to go?" How about, "Why don't you go out with your girlfriends while I clean the house?" Wouldn't it be nice to hear, "Honey, I got a big bonus and I want you to redo our house. If this doesn't do it I'll give you more."

What about hearing your man say, "Hey, Babe, while I am on that long boring business trip, why don't you take five or six of your girlfriends on a Caribbean cruise or maybe Vegas?" Or perhaps, "Why don't you and a girlfriend go to the South of France and rent us a three- or four-bedroom vacation home?" Or possibly, "Babe, why don't you rent a large boat for a huge fund-raiser for that charity of yours?" Maybe your guy might say, "Here is five thousand towards a new fall wardrobe." That would NEVER happen at my home as we aren't "in the money." But one can dream.

Okay, maybe you can change your man by changing yourself. Yeah, sure. I frankly think it is pretty much impossible to change another person, especially if they don't want to change. Women are probably a lot easier to change than men.

I have two girlfriends that tried to change their husbands.

Now they are both divorced.

Need I say more? Don't think so. Ask for God's guidance and for a lot of patience. My sister said the smartest thing I ever said was, "Marriage isn't easy." No kidding, you both have to work at it. A woman spending too much money or not compromising ended it for a couple of guys I know.

Chapter 31 *Fun downtown*

Recently, I met an attractive gal (forty or so) at a bookstore signing. We talked about my books. She asked me if her eighty-five-year-old mom would like it. I asked if she was a fun gal. She said, "Sort of" (whatever that means). I told her I had a few words that could offend some people but hasn't offended most. I only use these words occasionally. Okay, what are they? – shit, damn, hell and bitch. Then she made this conversation surprising when saying, "I might give it to my mom on the sly, as my dad censors everything first." I said, "You've got to be kidding," She said, -"I'm glad I'm not the only one who finds this weird. Unbelievable in this century but Mom will be eighty-five and grew up in a very different time." I'm not that far away in age, but, man, I find that unbelievable and yes, weird, weird, weird!

My "with it" friend Viv, who is close to ninety, thought it was really unbelievable when I told her. Viv is an awesome gal. She keeps her hair red, nails done, wears a size ten (sharp clothes a forty-year old would love), wears sharp-looking shoes and coordinates her jewelry, still works in her flower beds, keeps her home clean, plays bridge, reads most of the current top sellers and is a LOT of fun! (Read more about her in *Hold on to Your Panties and Have Fun.*)

I find book signing a fun event because I love, love, love people. I love having fun with all kinds of gals and guys. At a recent signing I was joking around with an older couple that I thought had been married a long time. I winked at her as I said," You know you could have done better." They both laughed as she said, "I don't think so." He said," You could have married Bill." She said," Who?" He said, "That baldheaded guy you dated". "Oh, no, I would never have married him." I said, "At least this one has hair even though he could be better looking." They laughed. Then I said, "You may not realize that I am the female version of Don Rickles." They laughed again. What a cute, fun couple, who obviously love one another a lot. Theirs is probably a second marriage. It could be as he mentioned her dating a bald man, right? If you marry a man with hair, he has a chance of keeping it, maybe? If he is a bright, good-looking and educated man – so much the better. If he is an honest, hard-working and a good guy who doesn't do drugs or overdrinks, even better!

P.S. Wonder if the old control freak censors his wife's speech?? Man, oh man, had the older couple come with the daughter and he said anything negative, believe me – I would have put that "ass" in his place! Oh yes, FYI, I might have told him that he was behind the times and how dare he treat his wife like that. To tell the truth, I probably would have been so shocked, I probably would not have replied. How dare a man in 2015 act like that? In the early 1900s I don't think my grandmothers would have put up with such a thing.

Chapter 32 *Fun Stopping A Train*

Have you ever heard the phrase "You're so ugly you could stop a train?" Well, baby, I have! No kidding, I have!

Actually, I was at a friend's book launch. She had just finished reading from her book when all of a sudden the door opened and in walked a favorite person, the owner of the restaurant a couple of doors down. She said, "Does anyone own a red van parked next to my restaurant?" "I do," I said. "Well, you had better move it as the sheriff is getting ready to tow it off." I hurried down the sidewalk praying I would arrive in time. Hubby was out of town. What if I am too late? Oh, Lord, Hubby will not be happy! I arrived "in time"; however, the sheriff was there, standing next to my van. He was not happy. I said, "I am so sorry." I moved my van closer to the building, away from the train track as I see the engineer glaring at me! Again, I mouth, "I am so sorry." Walking back to the bookstore I started grinning as I remember the old saying, "She's so ugly she could stop a train." Then I looked up and said, "Well, Mother, too bad you didn't live long enough to see that!"

What happened about two years later was really surprising. The train actually hit and totaled the van of the gal who had alerted me. She definitely is NOT ugly enough to stop a train – in fact, she is an attractive middle-aged gal.

Have you ever stopped a train?

Chapter 33 *Fun With Doughnuts*

What has no beginning, no end, and a hole? You guessed it! A doughnut (or a circle or a zero.)

When I was about five years old I remember a truck coming to our home – full of all kinds of doughnuts and pastries. They were on sliding wooden shelves that the man pulled out for my mother to select her goodies. I remember her being very fond of long custard-filled chocolate éclairs. I also remember a few flies floating around – not cool.

Through the years I have sampled many different doughnuts, cookies, and cakes, as my hips certainly show. My brother didn't call me "fat ass" for nothing, baby.

There were small powdered cake doughnuts as well as chocolate ones. There were those with sprinkles although I personally never favored those. There were twisted doughnuts and doughnuts with nuts on top, and some with sprinkles (ugh).

At Halloween time we now find pumpkin doughnuts in various designs on the grocer's shelves. Do you love those jelly-filled?

I read where there is a Chicago Smell and Taste Temperament and Research Foundation that did a study of six hundred doughnuts. They found out that certain personality types choose specific doughnuts. If you are a jelly girl, chances are you probably have a strong personality who may be assertive and very confident. You were probably a born leader. I read about this study in one of my favorite magazines, "Woman's World." I adore this magazine which I pick up as a reward for going grocery shopping. This article did not mention my very favorite doughnut – Krispy Kreme's cream filled with chocolate glaze. I have frequently been chosen leader in many groups; however, I am not a fan of the jelly filled.

The next doughnut they talked about is another favorite of mine – glazed doughnuts with chocolate icing. Dr. Hirsch, who headed up this study, says, "Chocolate lights up our reward centers in our brains, boosting our moods." I say

"Yeah" to any chocolate, how about you? If you love these too, you are probably outgoing and a true friend. Dr. Hirsch says these fun types are party ready. Yes, we are! If you prefer Boston cream you may be highly intuitive and are sensitive to your family and friend's needs.

If you especially like powdered doughnuts you are a kid-at-heart that smiles a lot and can be a lot of fun. These doughnuts remind me of my early childhood so they are in my top four.

Sprinkles-doughnut lovers are said to be serene intellectuals that have a flashy side. They dream up ideas as varied as the sprinkles. Frankly, I can walk by these, can you? In fact, I hate very few things but I hate sprinkles. Yes, I do. To me they have no taste and are gritty.

If you like plain doughnuts you most likely have "high moral standards," simple values, are honest and work hard. If you are a complex, confident person? Chances are you are a fan of crullers and their pinwheel shape.

The last doughnut seems to me to be the people's favorite – the glazed. At least I have seen a lot of kids selling big boxes of them for fund-raising events in the South. The one I remember was Krispy Kreme, not surprising as they are a Southern company and an all-time Southern favorite.

My sister and I both love maple icing on cream-filled doughnuts although Dr. Allen Hirsch did not include these or my very favorite, the chocolate iced cream-filled. Why? Don't know.

Who pays for these doughnut and cookie studies? Although interesting, couldn't money go to a better cause? Just asking...

P.S. Look for more information on insights into your personality in the favorite cookie chapter.

P.P.S. I heard they had a doughnut throw-down on the food channel.

Interesting???

My friend Leslie gave me this doughnut recipe:

Fun and Easy Doughnuts

2 T. white vinegar • ½ t. baking soda

3/8 c. milk • ½ t. salt

2T. shortening • ½ t. vanilla

½ c. sugar • 2 c. sifted all-purpose flour

1 egg • 1 qt. oil for frying

Mix vinegar into the milk. Let sit until thick while preparing other ingredients. Mix shortening with sugar and beat until smooth. Mix in the egg and vanilla until well blended. Sift flour, baking soda and salt, then stir into the sugar mixture, alternating with the vinegar and milk. Roll dough on a floured board until 1/3-inch thick. Use doughnut cutter to form doughnuts. Let dough wait about ten minutes while oil is heating to 375 degrees in a large deep skillet. Fry doughnuts in oil. When they become golden, turn once. Drain on paper towels. While warm dust with cinnamon mixed with a small amount of brown sugar or powdered sugar.
Enjoy!

P.P.P.S. I was amazed watching a recent food show called something like "Doughnut Challenge." The two finalists had to use dinner food as inspiration for three different doughnuts. The chef who won added bacon plus some form of a sugar mixture to, of all things, a bagel. Hey, people, a bagel is a bagel, IT IS NOT A DOUGHNUT!!!

According to "Woman's World," the best doughnuts are: The Voodoo Doughnut, in Portland, Oregon. The shop's namesake treat oozes raspberry jelly and is staked with a pretzel stick. In Chicago, you can get glazed and infused doughnuts that have a mixture of chocolate and vanilla cake covered with frosted cream cheese and red velvet crumbs. In Somerville, Massachusetts, you can get a Union Square doughnut. It is covered in maple syrup frosting and bacon chunks and has all the flavors of breakfast wrapped up in one. Philadelphia, Pennsylvania, has a Federal doughnut that is blueberry and tastes like a stack of fresh-from-the-skillet flapjacks. Washington, D.C., has an Astro doughnut that is a play on crème brulée. It has a crunchy five-torched glaze with a vanilla custard center. Of course, a well-known favorite is from New Orleans, Louisiana and made in the famous Cafe du Monde. Piping hot beignets are squares of fried dough and are blanketed with powdered sugar. The last doughnut on the list is from Houston, Texas. It is known as a Shipley Do-Nut. They are light fluffy yeast donuts covered with a cherry-sugar icing.

P.P.P.S. Doughnuts became popular in the 1920s after the doughnut machine was invented by Adolph Levitt, a Jewish refugee.

Chapter 34 *Fun At Christmas*

Memories of holidays surface at this time of year. When I was about nine years old I remember a big Christmas. This was during World War II when my Aunt Helen lived with us. Her husband, Paul, was stationed in Japan, where he was a cook in the Army.

My mother and Aunt Helen made us new clothes from fabric by hand. Not sure if fabric was rationed or not – clothes, I believe, were. Shoes and sugar definitely were in short supply due to the war. I remember my mother and Aunt Helen staying up late sewing, so we didn't see what we were to be given. Some of our new clothes were made from feed sacks. (Chicken feed came in these sacks.) It was exciting if we got two or three matching sacks, which meant there would be enough fabric for an adult's or young girl's dress. The sacks were taken apart and washed and ironed before being made into garments. Smaller pieces were made into blouses, aprons, pot holders and doll clothes. The fabric was durable; however, a bit rough.

I'm not sure just what my brother received that Christmas, but my sister and I really "took home the bacon," so to speak. I remember waking up so excited to see what Santa brought me. Before Christmas vacation my friends were telling me there wasn't a Santa. I told them what my mother told me. "If you don't believe he doesn't come to see you." After Christmas our parents asked my brother and me to sit down because they had something to tell us. Learning the truth about Santa was a sad and shocking end to my childhood! I was almost ten years old. Sidebar: I was near the top of my class so I wasn't stupid. I just wanted to believe. Fast-forward light years ahead to when I was a mom of a nearly five year old and a son almost two. At Eastertime we put out the boys' Easter baskets on the screened-in porch. When his little brother was napping Scott said, "Mommy, it is ridiculous to think that the Easter bunny hops over the fence and opens up the porch door to bring in our Easter baskets. You and Daddy are the Easter bunny, right?" Sidebar: It isn't easy raising really smart kids. I told him, "You're right, but if you tell your brother or any other kid you know – guess what? – you won't be getting any Easter candy ever." While Scott was out playing I told my Hubby what had happened. I said, "Be prepared, he may ask you about Santa. I'm not sure what you want to say but I want him to stay a believer a couple of more years." That afternoon, sure enough, Scott asked his dad. Hubby, never one to lie, said, "Santa is the spirit of Christmas." Scott brought the subject up with me. I told him, "A lot of kids don't believe in Santa, so guess what? He doesn't bring them gifts." My son said that when Santa had come the year before, he had noticed that he wore the same shoes that his grandpa wore. My dad had dressed up as Santa and one of his high-topped shoes had a lift. I was surprised Scott noticed at age four. I told him Santa had a lot of helpers and that they wore different kinds of shoes. I went on to tell him Christmas is special, because it is Christ's birthday and that is why we give gifts to others. I told him Santa has the giving spirit, but wouldn't come to kids who didn't believe. Knowing him to be a bit greedy, he would pretend to believe, and he did.

We never made Santa's gifts or Christmas giving to our children a really big deal. Probably because I had been so disappointed and really embarrassed when I went back to school and listened to the other kids. Each year we put two or three items unwrapped on either side of the tree for each of our boys. Anything else we gave them was wrapped and from Dad and Mom. We never ran charge cards up to be regretted later. We gave the kids clothes at Easter, start of school, for Christmas and a few summer t-shirts and shorts. They usually got a joint family game and one or two toys.

In later years – when they were pre-teens and teens, we might give them what we called a "Ho Ho." Now it would be called a "Ha Ha." We always told them it was a Ho Ho before they unwrapped it. It might be a used garage sale game or something they had lost and I found, or a food item. Something fun or funny. Usually the item – like the big can of beans, I gave my brother when he was sixteen. Sidebar: My brother ALWAYS guessed every gift. I fixed him. I wrapped up the can with newspaper, rolling it until it was huge. I added rocks and big screws in empty Coke cans to make noise, and put them in a big box. It rattled, etc. I did the same with about fifteen cans of beans for my brother's sixtieth or seventieth birthday. He loved all the beans. He even wrote me a very funny and rather crude poem after receiving his "gift."

Of all the lovely Christmas celebrations we have had, one of the war years stands out, as we loved having Aunt Helen with us. The tree was big with multicolored lights and tinsel, which Mother loved, plus old ornaments. It was beautiful! The mound of gifts around it has never been equaled. I remember that every year our paternal grandparents always gave me a puzzle (always beyond me) and a hanky. I never liked puzzles and remember complaining to my dad. He said, "You have to think of the love behind the gift, not the gift itself." My paternal grandparents were Quakers and very conservative. I feel sorry for people who get so carried away buying stuff for their kids. Perhaps they want to give the gifts they never had. I get a little carried away now with my girls, daughter in-love and granddaughter-in-love. I love giving gifts to them since I never had daughters. Thankfully their husbands seem to understand. From time to time I meet another author who writes a book I think one of my guys might like. I get one autographed for them. Our son S.C. loved my friend Bill Kinnick's book *Sanctuary* and was so happy to meet him at my big-ass birthday party.

Chapter 35 *Fun With Dogs and Surviving Allergies*

This chapter was previously printed in The Dalmatian Club of America's magazine, "The Spotter"

- Do not allow the dog in your bedroom.
- Do not allow the dog on your furniture.

- Do not allow the dog to lick your face or arms.
- Wash hands after handling your dog.
- If possible, provide crate in laundry room, hopefully away from your bedroom – a portable air filter helps.
- Wash bedding often – weekly for sure. (I use small amount of detergent and dry bleach with warm water.)
- Vacuum floors, carpet and rugs often.
- Change vacuum bag frequently.
- During pollen season, use dog wipes or damp rag to wipe dog before he comes in the house.
- Give dog weekly shower or bath. This is a good time to clean ears, cut nails and check your dog over.
- Vacuum in and under crate weekly.
- Have your vent system cleaned every few years. You may also want to get an air filter that attaches to your furnace system. Be sure to check and change any air filters frequently.
- You may want to use Borax (found in laundry aisle) or baby powder on dog bedding to keep doggie odor down.
- When traveling, shake and turn over bedding often. Take extra bedding and trash bag for dirty ones.

If you have to – take allergy medicine or shots. I took allergy shots for forty-two years. Now I take 12-hour Allegra D or another 12-hour antihistamine/decongestant twice daily. You may want to try over-the-counter Zicam Extreme Congestion Nasal Gel. I have found both very helpful. Both are available at your local drugstore. It is a small price to pay for the love of a good dog.

P.S. Living with allergies and your dog is not easy. But nothing worthwhile in life is ever easy, is it?

Chapter 36 *Fun at Easter*

Most of this chapter was written by Emily's youngest son, T. J. Hoover

Our oldest son at almost five said to me, "Mommy, it is ridiculous to think that the Easter Bunny jumped over our big fence, (five feet) opened the porch door to put the Easter baskets on the porch. (It was raining) You and Daddy are the Easter bunny aren't you?" "Yes, we do your Easter baskets but if you tell your little brother or anybody you won't get any more eggs or chocolate candy." So he played along.

Easter, I feel, should be a joyful holiday as Christ died for us that we might be forgiven. Years ago I attended an Easter service at a Unity church where the woman minister wore a very shiny gold suit. It was shiny like a figure-skater might wear, which I found a bit shocking. She had taken joy to a new level.

Our younger son, T.J. Hoover, is an Episcopal minister. He sent me his Easter sermon. The scripture reading was from the book of Matthew and is as follows:

"After the Sabbath, as the first day of the week was dawning, Mary Magdalene and the other Mary went to see the tomb. And suddenly there was a great earthquake; for an angel of the Lord, descending from heaven, came and rolled back the stone and sat on it. His appearance was like lightening and his clothing as white as snow. For fear of him the guards shook and became like dead men. But the angel said to the women, 'Do not be afraid; I know you are looking for Jesus who was crucified. He is not here; for he has been raised, as he said. Come, see the place where he lay. Then go quickly and tell his disciples, "He has been raised from the dead and indeed he is going ahead of you to Galilee; there you will see him." This is my message for you.' So they left the tomb quickly with fear and great joy, and ran to tell his disciples. Suddenly Jesus met them and said, 'Greetings!' And they came to him, took hold of his feet, and worshiped him. Then Jesus said to them, 'Do not be afraid; go and tell my brothers to go to Galilee; there they will see me.'"

The ABCs of Easter

"Adam, the new Adam's 'Jesus' is absent from the tomb. For the two Mary's, this is their first Easter. The Alpha or the beginning of Easter and the beginning of a new life for them. An Angel appeared, perhaps the same Angel as in Advent, according to Luke, the Angel said to the shepherds: 'DO NOT BE AFRAID.' The anxious, apprehensive Mary's had been grieving for their anointed one – Jesus – was absent or missing from the cave. Abandonment. Bewildered, they had lost their beloved and they didn't have enough belief when Jesus had told them that he would arise. The angel told them: 'DO NOT BE AFRAID' and shortly later Jesus would tell them the same: 'DO NOT BE AFRAID.' For now, the biggest 'A' word in this story is AFRAID. I want you to imprint this into your hard drive for those unexpected moments in your life when you need help: 'DO NOT BE AFRAID.' The opposite of fear is hope and there is hope when the doctor first utters the C word – 'CANCER.'

"The Angel in a sense absolved their fears, helped them go from the utter darkness of the soul, from the night turning into day as it was dawn. The Angel helped them to align themselves with a new reality, a new spirit, a new consciousness, a new energy, a new freshness and a new Alpha. "Like an Italian sports car, in six seconds these women turned from anxiety, to utter profound belief.

"The Angel ushered them off quickly to spread the good news. God didn't pick the first-born male disciples to be the first Preachers, or alpha Preachers. These two Mary's joyfully, joyfully they adored him and preached for the first time, the very first Easter Sermon: 'He is not here he has risen!' Now we get to the most important 'A' word –'Alleluia'!
So much better than 'Afraid'!

"For our scientific minds, this supernatural story is hard for us to believe, our knowledge belittles the super naturalness. The Gospels are full of the grisly details of the Passion. However, there are little details of those three days, only what the two Mary's were feeling. The science of the story is not important.

"The bindings, the clothes that draped, entombed both Jesus and Lazarus are symbolic of what binds us – anxiety, depression, guilt, shame, intolerance and all the isms, racism, nationalism, in short – SINs. In verse nine, Jesus's first word to them was 'Greetings' but in some Bibles it is: 'Behold'! We are the ones entombed, bound beckoning for a new and perfect world. We beckon for a new life. Believe that life is here for you to behold for you to just be, just be in it and go beyond bountifully and become a believer in 'C' as in Christ. 'C' for crucified. 'C' for compassion. 'C' for community. 'C' for cuddling. Cuddle up with Christ. Have courage, commitment and Care to do the very best in life, in your work and in your community with your children and with your companions.
Center yourself. Celebrate, Care, we are the Church!
"For those of you who are new here, we are honored and glad that you have come into our lives this day, Easter Day to celebrate in your heart, your cardiac center and in your brain cortexes. We didn't call you to come this day. You were called to count your life mathematically and hopefully the pluses;

whether you have been naughty or nice, as in Christmas, hopefully your pluses account for more than your minuses; for when it's your Omega day, judgement day, that will be your Easter and it will be a celebration with Jesus, tied to his resurrection. Angels will assist you. Your beloved companions will greet you with open arms, welcoming you to the eternal community of Christ. The music of heavenly choirs beckons your ears. Your eyes will see the most brilliant kaleidoscope of true color, beauty of unimaginable dreams. Complete perfection. Complete love enfolds, surrounds you, and heals you. No more rust, decay, oxidation and disease. For in heaven, our overburdened, overtaxed body has been lifted. Lifted high. We have had our cross to bear and Jesus showed us the way, proudly, courageously. Lift high the cross for he has risen. We go back to the wonderful beginning, the Alpha then to the Omega. The circle of life is complete now and we know we will join our friend, Jesus. So DO NOT BE AFRAID. Easter is here for you and for me!

"Alleluia Alleluia! Amen."

Chapter 37 *Fun In Cleveland*

If you're from Cleveland, Ohio, you may still be upset with the formerly beloved basketball star LeBron James, who a few years ago left Cleveland for Miami. Now everyone is "in love" with one of the most dynamic point guards, Kyrie Irving. Hey, folks, basketball is big, big, big in Ohio!!!

There is an old saying, "If you don't like the weather in Cleveland, wait fifteen minutes and it will change." Growing up in Ohio and attending The OSU, I had several roommates and some other OSU friends from the Cleveland area; visiting them I have experienced Cleveland weather.

Summer is pleasant enough but unfortunately it doesn't last long. There is not much of a spring or fall. Winter is, for the most part miserable. So why, oh why would LeBron James want to go to sunny Miami for more money? We'll see what Kyrie Irving is made of when he becomes a free agent in 2016. You have to be a strong person to put up with all the winter storms, baby.

It can be beautiful and picturesque as I saw recently flying into Cleveland in the middle of a snowstorm. It was like being in the middle of a snow globe. It was so peaceful and the homes looked "Christmas card" perfect. After attending my brother-in-law's funeral, in mid-December, we noticed how fast the snow was falling and how bad the back roads were becoming. Driving west, about one hundred miles, my son and I found the highway being shoveled and iced. The drive back took twice as long. Not only that, we saw three cars in the ditch and two more being towed. Why, oh why would anyone want to work in Miami for more money??? I would love to go back to the Akron and Cleveland area to see relatives and I would love to go to the Rock and Roll Hall of Fame. It would be fun to go to Kelly's Island and the Sandusky and Cleveland art museum. As I remember, the one in Cleveland has a large awesome Monet. Although I adored the Monet in Chicago a bit more. But, baby, I would only want to go to Ohio in the summer!!!

I can't blame LeBron James for leaving Ohio, as Miami is the place I would go. He had an audience in Cleveland who appreciated him. Now Florida fans appreciate him, and add the sun and beach, sounds good to me. Sorry, Cleveland – get over it.

P.S. Now LeBron is back doing well in Cleveland. Apparently, Cleveland fans are forgiving after all.

P.P.S. I loved the gourmet food and the people at the Marriott Airport Hotel. Fun, Fun! I'll see you next summer – maybe.

P.P.S. In 2018 LeBron is leaving Cleveland for Los Angeles. If I were a betting woman, I would have told you I believed that to be a done deal. I heard on TV in the summer or fall of 2017 that LeBron was seen working out and doing hoops with "The Lakers". I also read that LeBron has a house there. Ok Cleveland fans, he is from Akron, not Cleveland, ok!

Chapter 38 Fun Getting and Keeping a Job

Frankly, I've made a few career errors in my life. However, I have also learned some things. The most important fact is not to quit a job unless you have another one lined up. Very important is don't bad-mouth anyone or the company at any time even if you want to leave. (At least I didn't do the latter.) Before taking another position, research the new company and be prepared to tell the new H.R. person why you want to work at their company. For instance, you know the new place has an excellent reputation. You also feel you would like to grow with them. Be prepared to tell them what you can contribute and how you are prepared to work hard to make this happen. There is a recent new book I suggest you get from Amazon.com or the library, *Yes! The Job is Mine – 4 Steps To Get The Job*, by Terry Patrick Walton. I hear it tells you how to shine in the interviews, how to grow your own network, and help you land the job.

I recently read an article in "Glamour Magazine" by Lauren Chan, titled "How to Dress for the Job You Want: The New Rules." She points out that you need different looks for different positions. For her interview for a fashion editor she wore polished dark gray pants, black top and a dark metallic classic leather jacket. She added high heel sandals and a tote like shoulder bag. She states that most people make judgements in fourteen seconds of meeting someone new. For different jobs people wear different looks. A fashion editor dresses very differently than someone wanting to teach first-graders or yoga. Author Chan pulled up "Glamour" online and looked to see how the executives were dressed. Another idea is to cruise by the place to see what employees are wearing as they go to or from work. If the gals have on flats and are carrying large bags, they could have heels to wear at work. Chan maintains that a fifty-mm-pump (whatever that is) in black is the preferred work shoe. Put your heels on before entering the building for your interview. According to the American Orthopedic Foot and Ankle Society, the women with more education wear lower heels.

Interesting?

Other interview hints:

• Make sure your make-up is not overdone.

• Be well groomed, clean and have your clothes well pressed.

• Avoid skirts that are short unless you are trying out to be a pole dancer, Ha Ha.

• Skirt length should be long enough that skin isn't touching a chair when you are seated.

• Don't wear heels if you aren't used to them.

• Carry a large neat and tidy tote bag instead of carrying several bags.

• Plan to arrive early.

• Even in the heat of summer wear a light jacket. It should help you with your confidence, as well as it looks professional.

- If low on money consider thrift shops. I got a top designer jacket for under twenty dollars.
- Try to project "the best you" by checking your makeup, check your teeth (Leftover salad doesn't help you.). Ask yourself, "Would I like to meet this person I see in the mirror?"
- And don't forget to extend your hand with a bright shiny smile. To keep your job, show up ten minutes early and stay at least a few minutes longer every day. Dress for success by always looking your best.

Try really hard to learn as much as you can every day. Always be friendly without getting caught up in office gossip. If someone is saying negative comments about anyone, refuse to comment. If possible say, "I remember there is something I have to do." Or perhaps a phone call or, if at lunch, excuse yourself to wash your hands.

Experts advise you to try to dress up a level. (You don't need a great deal of clothes if you coordinate your separates.) By always projecting a good image, working hard and keeping out of office politics you could be on your way to a successful career.

If you are unhappy ask yourself if you are expecting too much. I have often seen spoiled gals blame others for everything that goes wrong. You need to listen to comments and criticisms given you. Don't try to defend yourself. Really listen. Then say, "Do you really think so?" If they say, "Yes" – work on yourself. Don't be a crybaby.

God didn't promise us the right to be happy all the time. Happiness on the job or at home is most often having the right attitude. If you need help with this, talk to your doctor or minister. Someone said, "Happiness is a lack of sadness." Think positive, help others and good things will follow. May God bless you with the wisdom to make the right decisions.

Chapter 39 *Fun With Handbags and Purses*

Every season the fashion experts come up with "new looks" in clothing, bags, shoes, make-up and hair styles. This could drive us crazy if we let it. Maybe that is why I go for a more classic look with "pops" of the new trends when I'm updating my wardrobe.

Some women are, in my opinion, a bit obsessed with either bags or shoes. A gal I know has a closet full of bags in bags. That is the way the expensive bags are sold. They come with or you can buy matching accessories. My question is, how many bags does a gal need?

Frankly, I feel we need a few bags but not a closet full. For any guy reading this, you need to know that we need a casual bag to carry when we are in jeans and a very different look for a formal evening event. We need a larger bag for work or every day. We may want to carry a laptop, work-related papers and gym clothes for workouts. I saw an article with photographs about what a celebrity carried. Her bag contained lipstick, make-up, reading glasses, tissues, a wallet and a bottle of vitamins.

My girlfriend Judy told me what she totes around. She says, "I carry everything you would possibly need including credit cards, reading glasses, sunglasses, toothpicks, hair combs, breath mints, receipts, Kleenexes, cell phone and other incidentals from time to time. I have also taken to carrying tweezers in case a friend needs a chin hair plucked! I have four purses which have dust covers and thanks for reminding me... it's time to bring out the fall-looking Louis Vuitton which I keep covered and in its own box. This is just in case someone steps into my closet and just happens to notice I really do have one! I don't bother to tell them I bought it from a friend, used!" What a fun gal!

She told me she has about forty bags. Another friend who likes to own the latest bags often takes her older ones to a resale shop or gives to a friend. She gave me one and it was just like new. Very generous and sweet, isn't she?

Then there was my Dal friend, Cheryl, who died about two years ago. I asked her husband, Buddy, if he had emptied her purse yet. He said, "No." I asked him to, then call me and tell me what he found. It contained a cell phone, a notepad, her business cards, fifteen other people's business cards, sunglasses and case, pills, eye make-up with a mirrored case, hand sanitizer, a Dalmatian zippered coin case, dental floss, moist towel-lets, drops for contacts, wrapped candy, J.C. Penney and Macy's gift cards, a restaurant gift card, Renew skin cream, $159, a voter's registration and auto insurance cards, driver's license, credit cards, eleven reward cards, photo of a Dalmatian on a motorcycle, Kleenex, emery boards, sticky notes in a covered container, a checkbook, four pens, green, black and two blue, with rubber bands around them, zippered case with breath mints, lipstick, breath spray, Tums, eyeglass cleaner, chap stick, eyebrow pencil, safety pins, gum, Purina Pro Plan information, calendar, handicapped parking permit and medical notebook. Buddy was surprised at the money and gift cards. I told him to go out and buy himself some new clothes. Because of my back issues I carry only my wallet, a bottle of water, tissue, a small medicine case for my allergy pills, wet wipes, a pen, reading and sunglasses. Isn't that enough? (Some people would call me a "light weight," until they see my hips!)

Back to types of bags, there are small wallet type bags, clutches, simple small bags and then there are large tote bags.

Some of these are artistic marvels with hand painting. Then there are larger bags with lots of brass bling or maybe a lot of fringe or glitz. Inside most bags are pockets for your cell phone, lipstick and keys. Sometimes they have a center zip pocket which some gals, like my mother, really liked. I find those bags drive me crazy as I can't remember where anything is. These bags don't have a north or south or left or right so how can you find anything? Of course, I have to admit I sometimes mess up my nail polish trying to find something in a larger bag. Is there no hope for me? Old age and messy nails – that's how it is – for this old bitch. My favorite bag is a pewter, very lightweight leather one made by "The Sac." It was on sale four or five years ago and still is decent looking after being used ninety percent of the time. It goes with everything! A practical choice for me. Note to younger gals, life is easier if you don't change bags often.

If you can carry more items than you have toes, you will be putting a lot of strain on your back. This will catch up with you. Back pain, once it starts is very difficult to completely get rid of, so please take care of what God gave you. Ask yourself, "Is my back health important?" If so, have most often used items in your bag. Have a box in your car with the rest of your stuff so if you really need it, you will have it near. Trust me – my friends Cheryl and Judy really won't use all that stuff every time they go out. You could keep a work bag and add a small clutch with your lipstick, meds, wallet, note pad and pen that could be removed for going to lunch or to run into the grocery store. Always keep your bag out of sight in your car and remember to lock your car up.

Where do you store your bags? I use an antique wood "hall tree" that is painted white. In some houses I have had coat hooks put on the side wall of my closet or in some cases I had shelves. You could go to a big box store and get fabric shelves that hang in your closet next to your clothes or store them in clear plastic boxes with labels that sit on your closet floor. You could also put a few hooks on the side wall of your closet or on the back of your closet door or store them in a large plastic container under the bed. Regardless, about once a year, go through them and sell, consign or give away those you aren't using. Recycle please, baby.

Chapter 40 Fun With John Wayne and Other Cowboys

Did I know John Wayne? No, but I have had fun watching him on the big and little screens. I've always loved tall good looking muscular men. No, I don't think that's why I married one. Well, he is tall, but never a muscle guy. But I can dream, can't I?

Frankly, I have had a LOT of fun teasing guys. I even had a shorter (than me) guy who apparently had the hots for me. No matter their height – there are fun guys, and those not so much fun. Then there are guys who THINK they are fun and funny but they aren't. Or I don't find them funny. I've been watching The "Last Comic Standing." I find Roseanne Barr fun and funny; however, what I didn't find funny are a LOT of the comics in 2014. Yet I heard Roseanne's distinctive laugh in the background. Humor is different for everyone, isn't it?

I loved Johnny Carson and his funny retorts. I loved, loved, loved how fast Joan Rivers could give "it" back, which I feel is a gift. I hear that I am pretty good at that, too. However, kids, even though I feel I could keep up with most, I know Joan would have been a real challenge. I would have liked to have met her. What a loss for us all. QVC is still selling new things she has designed. I recently bought a handsome faux leather Chanel inspired quilted red jacket that I adore. I have an old knee-length black trench raincoat I still receive compliments on, as well as several other pieces I love. Like Joan, I wear a lot of black and red. (The trench is still available.)

Another fun person I would like to meet is Blake Shelton. My type of man except for the possible over-drinking. I love his sense of humor and his manly good looks. Then there is Jesse Palmer. What a hottie. He seems like he would be fun, fun, fun!

A man without humor is like a house without furniture. (How do you like that? I made it up.)

To me, a "good man" is one who is emotionally and financially responsible and of course has a sense of humor. Good looks are like the icing on the cake. One of my college roommates who attended a very large high school told me it was the high school nerds who became most successful in life. She told me after having attended a fortieth class reunion that these nerds not only were financially doing well, but also had long-term marriages. In college I dated a future physicist and several engineers. I also hung out with my now Hubby's frat brothers – most engineering students. Most of these genius type guys were average-looking and needed a woman to help them select their clothes.

My Hubby hung out with the upper-classmen. When the older guys celebrated their twentieth graduation anniversary, we were also invited and had a great time! One of the more social guys organized everything. We met at the Triangle

House (OSU, of course) for cocktails, followed by a trip to a cool Bar B Q place. The next day we all went to the alumni House where we met Archie Griffin, former Ohio State University football star and twice Heisman winner, who had become the alumni "Big Cheese" – Head of O.S.U. alumni or some such title. Sidebar: A year ago I met one of Archie's girlfriend's roommates at my garage sale – small world. We took a bus tour of the campus and got to go behind the scenes at the then new stadium. After a nice lunch, a walk around Mirror Lake and a trip to an Ohio State University memorabilia store, we met again later for more cocktails and a banquet. Everyone was dressed up for this lovely dinner. After we ate, the guys took turns around the table and caught everyone up on what work, etc., they had done since college. WOW, those twenty-five or thirty guys turned out to be "movers and shakers" in their various fields of engineering. They each introduced their wife or guest. It was really interesting to me as I had not only dated my now Hubby, but at one time, I had dated another "Triangle." Sidebar: This was a time after Hubby had graduated, moved to Florida and broken up with me. There was also a fond or interesting time when the "Triangles" had a "square-dance party." I remember being about the only person in my square who actually knew how to square-dance.

Electrical engineers are considered to be the smartest or just seem that way. I know my place in the "smart-order" of people. Even though I was told in high school I could go on to be a doctor, believe me "no one" said anything about me being smart enough to be an engineer. Just saying! As the engineers introduced their wives, they told how they had met – most on blind dates in college or through the wives of other engineers. They also told how many kids they had and where they had lived. It was all fun. It was interesting that I was the only wife they applauded for. Who knew I had fans? Very surprising, but, hey, I've always been very attracted to bright men and women. They are just so much more interesting, don't you think? (To read more about my dating life, read *Hold on to Your Panties and Have Fun*.) The engineers I've known have the most unusually bright wives. Engineers may not be (on the scale of one to ten, tens – looks-wise), but they are usually very reliable, honest and help provide a good living. They all tend to be guys that drive the same car for years, and dress only to cover their bodies but caring very little for fashion. Their careers often come first, before family or wife. But I have to tell you from the ones I know, they are there for you for the long haul. But what do I know, right?

P.S. See the chapter on dating and life advice for you young ones or those reentering the dating scene. Better you than me.

Chapter 41 Fun With shiny New Shoes

Is there anything more fun in the entire world than getting a great new pair of shoes? Most gals I know love a pair of cute or pretty shoes!

As my "Panties Book" readers already know, finding shoes has never been an easy process for me. Now in old age it is even more difficult. Why? Because as we age our feet change. They spread both in length and width. I have narrow feet as well as thin feet (from top to bottom). It is extremely difficult now that I need an eleven and a half AA with a five A heel. No one makes such a size so I have a few eleven B's; the rest are twelves. I do better with sandals that have adjustable straps. Most of my shoes are purchased from catalogs.

www.auditionsshoes.com and www.marylandsquare.com. Sometimes, I get lucky with shoes from HSN or QVC. It is not unusual to go to a large city shoe store where I try on six or seven pairs and only find one pair, if any, that I purchase. I can tell you IF they are not supportive and somewhat attractive, I'm not buying them.

What about you?

Sandals date back to the time of Christ. Aren't flip-flops a version of sandals? There are a lot of variations of them both, aren't there? I wore very simple flip-flops when my kids were young. Not great for a flat foot but cheap. Now there are very expensive wedges, trendy gladiator type and high-heel sandals. Have you noticed the gladiator type of shoes are not as weird-looking as when they became popular? We get used to changes. Then how about the ballet flats that Audrey Hepburn made popular. Aren't there still ballet flats that resemble the originals? I have a pair that are made of fabric in Campbell plaid, another pair in black and white hound's-tooth plus a pair in wine velvet and another pair – this time – with a square throat in black velvet. If you haven't worn fabric shoes, your toes don't know what they are missing.
They are so comfortable.

Oxfords are a more structured pre-sneaker type of tie shoe. High-top, early American type of tie shoes are seen today, primarily worn with the socks pulled over the top of the shoe. Sometimes gals wear them with leggings, turtlenecks and a big shirt, maybe plaid. Sometimes I've seen some of the stars wear canvas high-tops with tiger print jeans and a tee-shirt. For a spring/fall look there are also high oxfords with heavy soles made for hiking.

The wedge made its appearance in the forties on sandals, worn with shorts, pedal-pushers and sundresses.

They were also worn with playsuits that were one-piece cotton blouse/short pieces usually with a button front skirt worn open. Watch some of the old movies and you may see one of these gems in a picnic scene with a wedge sandal. Recently, I saw some suede wedge boots with lazor lace type work on the top of these boots. I saw them on Home Shopping Network (HSN) and actually ordered a pair for myself, for my daughter-in-love and granddaughter-in-love as Christmas gifts. One thing I like about HSN and QVC is that not only do they have good deals, if we don't like an item or in this case they don't fit, they are so easy to return. These are the first boots I have purchased in about ten years. I am in Florida in the winter and seldom have a chance to wear them. I ended up not keeping mine – they didn't fit, surprise, surprise. I have, also, seen a wedge bootie (a short boot) with an open toe. Not great looking in my opinion, but what do I know? Heels come in sandals of all types. Then there are the closed toe and heel classic types. If fashion calls for a pointy toe, go up a half to full size or you will mess up your toes and be miserable wearing them. Believe me, looking sexy may be fine when you are sitting – not when you are standing, walking or dancing. I love heels! Not the kill-your-back super five- or six-inch break-your-ankle type. I can see a very short gal wearing a four-inch but she should practice before wearing them out and be careful about how much she drinks.

I never had heels higher than two inches. Most women my age didn't either. Back when I was young they weren't available. My last heels were made of black faille fabric. They were a sophisticated Mary Jane style with a narrow strap and a button fastener. They had a French curved heel. (A French heel has a wider base where it joins the shoe and a little wider bottom with a lovely curve in-between.) Those heels were about one and a half inches and were worn for dinner dances and parties. Sadly, now my back won't allow me to wear them.

I have a very good girlfriend who showed me a picture of herself at her husband's funeral. (I believe I was on a cruise when he died.) Months later in the photo she sent me, I noticed her shoes. They were rounded open toe with an open heel of moderate height. She was wearing a nice church type dress. However, it was the shoes that got my attention. I said (always the bad girl that I am), "Wow, that's a surprise." She said, "What is?" I replied, "You were wearing 'bar-hopping' shoes to a funeral." "Really," she said. "Well, that's what I call them." She laughed – thank God. I didn't tell her some call them CFM shoes.

A local friend of mine sent me the following: "I put on a pair of striped cork wedges and was admiring them in the mirror with the outfit that matched perfectly. Looked great, until the cork broke in half while I was standing there doing nothing! Either the shoe was way too old and should have been tossed a long time ago or I have gained so much weight my shoes can't take it anymore. I prefer the first answer." Ha, ha.

When I was thirteen I had one pair of corrective shoes that were ugly, ugly, ugly!!! They were dog doo-doo brown oxfords with arch support. They also had wing-tips (like guy's shoes); plus they had little tiny holes all over. Oh, I forgot to tell you, they were size eleven AAAAA and had an inch-and-a-half heel, not cute saddle oxfords (white with black around the eyelets where the laces went with a narrow black strip at the heel that "the popular" girls were wearing, like Ellen wears on her show and Shirley Temple wore in "The Bachelor and The Bobby Soxer" movie). No wonder I resorted to humor. I had these ugly shoes until I was about twenty-four. They were very comfortable. (They were prescription shoes, from a doctor who my mother had taken me to, for my "back problems.") That's when I found out I had scoliosis, or curvature of the spine.

When I was sixteen my mother took pity on me and got me a pair of saddle oxfords which I wore to school, changing into the ugly shoes when I got home. I believe they were eleven AA, which required heavy socks. Man did I love them. At sixteen I started working part time in a shoe store and must have special-ordered summer heels. I don't remember what I wore to work at Dayton Power and Light where I worked as a lighting consultant, but I know I wore heels. A word about selling shoes. It is hard work with lots of bending and reaching. Kind of like my current Tai Chi classes. Plus you have to put up with gals who use you. Meaning they try on lots of shoes for fun – not always to buy. I did this for fifty-five cents an hour in 1952. I sold shoes until I left for Mary Washington College at which time I was getting sixty-five cents per hour. When I was seventeen Mother found, probably in the Penney's or Sears catalog, a pair of size ten black leather ballet flats to wear to the Junior/Senior Dance. They were uncomfortable but I wore them to formals throughout my freshman year of college. Finally, when I transferred to The Ohio State we found a pair of red high-heel sandals and I thought I was "hot stuff." About that time I also purchased a pair of black classy suede flats and a pair of black classic suede pumps. I know my mother must have felt sorry for me to put so much effort and money into these shoes. I had a friend send out an e-mail request asking my friends how many shoes they have. I also asked people and found out my buddies all seemed to be very blessed. I now have shoe bags on the back of my closet door and one on a narrow side wall in my closet. Sometimes I double up and put a pair of sandals in one of the slots instead of using two slots. I have shoes in North Carolina and Florida so I don't know for sure how many pairs I have. I am guessing about thirty pair – mostly sandals, plus two pair of boots (one red, one black) and two pair of heavy-duty sneakers I will probably pass on soon – too heavy. I knew I had accumulated a few extra pairs but was surprised at the amount when I started figuring it out. Each bag holds twelve pairs normally but I have seventeen in one bag here in North Carolina. Most of these I "tote," as my Southern friends say, back and forth from one home to another. Oh yes, I have two pair of sandals at the shoe repair shop here having the straps taken in to fit my narrow feet. Plus I have a pair of velveteen flats I seldom wear other than at Christmas time that I got when I was twenty-nine. They are old, old, old but still look good and still sort of fit.

This is one of the e-mail replies I got: "I have over two hundred pairs of shoes many of which I don't wear but hope to sometime! The shoes are everything from four pair of tennis shoes to dress heels which I rarely wear. I prefer summer sandals, flip-flops and comfortable flats." Is this gal blessed or what?

Most gals I talked to didn't know or didn't want to tell me how many they had. So, your guess is as good as mine. If they don't know – we know they have a few pairs.

What we do know is – gals love shoes, bags, girlfriends and sometimes even guys.

Chapter 42 Fun Boosting Your Energy Level

What I've found out through the years, when my energy level was low, is that often I needed to get blood tests to determine if my thyroid or potassium levels could be off. These are easily corrected with low-cost meds. (I speak from personal experience.) I had noticed for several months I had been dragging my butt. I was pushing myself to get basic chores done. Since I had just had my big-ass eightieth birthday, I thought it may be age-related. I called the doctor's office to see if I could get blood work done. I could and without an office visit. I had put off calling, believing I would have to go into the office. (Maybe they really don't want me to come in. Afraid of me? Hope so.) It had been about a year. I had been pushing myself with help from lots of herbs, vitamins and my energy drinks. Now, I can't believe how much more energy I have after a month on my upped thyroid meds.

Today I did a couple of loads of wash, tidied up the kitchen, exercised, washed my van by hand, ran several errands and have written two chapters. I tried on several pieces of clothing to see if I wanted to toss or keep. Oh yes, and I took care of Diva, the Dalmatian. Not bad for an old bitch – meaning me – however, Diva is eleven years old – so we're both old bitches. We have an ongoing contest to see who is going to die first.

If your blood tests are normal and you feel your energy level is not, it could be stress. If so, you may want to speak to your health care professional about taking Serine (which is an amino acid). This taken before bedtime may help. That along with avoiding television, cell phone and your computer use for an hour or two before bedtime. Empty your brain when preparing to sleep. Either take a warm bath, pray or take twenty minutes to relax. If you have worries – write them down. This sometimes reduces anxiety and insomnia.

I find I sleep better now that I try to get to bed by eleven o'clock and by making a list of things I need to do the next day. I release my concern over forgetting something important when I am in my morning fog. I have also found morning exercise helps. I try to use my fog time to get laundry going or to make phone calls. I drink a green tea caffeine energy drink, eat yogurt, with blueberries and a few nuts with my vitamins. I understand a three hundred to four hundred milligram dose of NOW (a health supplement brand EGCG) and green tea extract (Herb Com at about $10.00) is helpful, too. I haven't tried it yet. I do take a subliminal Ultra B-12 (NOW) that I feel gives me a boost. While there are a lot of very good vitamins I find that although quite pricey, I feel best when I take Life's Fortune (a multivitamin) along with a number of other supplements. I am blessed that I am able to pay to feel better. (Keep in mind, my van is thirteen years old – so no car payments.)

Back to you! If you wake up too early you may want to invest in blackout curtains, blinds or an eye mask. For noise control, as a light sleeper, I like my air filter which produces a mild white sound. I carry it wherever I travel.

For a drug alternative instead of sleeping pills you may want to try taking five hundred milligrams of thiamine, an amino acid, with three hundred twenty milligrams of magnesium, about an hour before going to bed. I read where a naturopathic doctor said that the combination helps people to relax and turn off the anxiety. To avoid the dreaded afternoon slump, the same doctor, recommended methyl vitamin B-12 in a one thousand milligram dose. B-12 boosts energy and increases serotonin which lifts your mood. One suggested was available for around seven dollars. (Jarrow Formula).

There are several mail-order sources for vitamins. I was turned on to Swanson Health Products (1-800-437-4148). You smart gals can check out others, I'm sure. The person who recommended Swanson said their prices were better than her employee discount at the health food store. I have found Swanson is slightly more than half the price of my local source. It goes without saying, eating more fruits and vegetables along with other healthy food choices, keeping our weight in the normal range and exercise keeps us healthier.

We probably are a lot happier, too.

It is up to you, sweetheart.

P.S. Reading fun and funny books can help as well as watching fun and funny films. (For your information, I hear pain is reduced when you are laughing.)

Chapter 43 *Fun Finding The One*

The quest for the perfect partner can take a long time and can involve heartbreak and pain. Someone said, "Don't marry the one you want to live with, but marry the one you can't live without." Better yet, the one who can't live without you!

I personally looked for a guy who had similar values and background. I wanted him to be smarter than me, the easy part, ha! Someone I was attracted to both physically and mentally. My dad served as a great role model. He was an engineer, kind, sweet, loyal and a Christian. He was brought up on a farm by loving yet very conservative parents. They were Quakers.

Side note: When I saw my grandmother cut the head off a chicken I decided that I WOULD NOT marry a farmer, although, while attending a rural high school I did date a couple. One of them that had liked me for several years, even told me, "College will ruin you." Oh my, that made me more determined to go.

My first proposal came from a hot sailor I met and dated while attending Mary Washington College in Fredericksburg, Virginia. The proposal shook me up. I was not going to give up my college years to be married – NO WAY.

We broke up.

Then I met a couple more guys at Ohio State that were fun, but I only went out with each a couple of times. Back in my dating days good girls did not put out until they were married. I would really think before going out with a guy more than twice. The engineer I married I dated because he was nice, fun and he was a gentleman. I met him through my roommate, who was dating his fraternity brother. We broke up several times. I would go back to dating a scientist that I liked a lot. I wanted to be a career woman. I didn't want to get married. Had "the pill" come out earlier, I may have moved in with one of these sweeties. I wanted to be a career woman, remember. Keep in mind I didn't know what kind of career woman. However, I still felt the pressure of society to get married. Remember, this was the fifties. After two years, my first Ohio State roommate had graduated from a two year dental hygienist program to marry her honey. He had graduated from dental school and would be a dentist in the Navy. Several other friends had gotten married as well as my younger cousin. Shortly before my engineer graduated, he broke up with me for the second time. A year later we were writing. Phone calls cost about forty to fifty dollars for about five minutes. There were no cell phones, e-mail or texts. He was working in Florida. I was working in Dayton, Ohio. We had broken up again a year earlier when he told me he had my ring but wasn't ready to give it to me. I said, "Fine, we'll both date." I did, he didn't. Why am I telling you this? To show you that life usually contains heartbreak on the way to true love.

Marriage and true love requires patience, understanding, compromise and hopefully, lots of good sex! The more common your background, the more common your values and the less likely the conflicts and misunderstandings.

Marriage is not easy and not for the faint of heart. Going to church together, I believe really helps as does a church family, working together for a common goal and always having each other's back.

Do what I say, not what I did, or do, or don't!

A young couple I know started out with a friendship in high school. She had a crush on him when he was a senior; she was a couple of years younger. He was in love (or maybe lust) with someone else. Ten years later he got a text from her. He traveled to her city for a class reunion. In the meantime she dated several guys which her family wasn't so fond of. They met again. A long-distance romance for six or seven months led to a move-in-together. Two years later they planned a wedding. He was thirty, she not yet twenty nine. (Very good ages for a successful marriage so statistics show.) These two have grandparents still married and parents together for centuries. Hopefully, they will have a long and happy life together. And hopefully you will too!

P.S. "You don't want to look back on the highway of your life and all you see is road kill." (Kathy Lee Gifford talking about Charlie Sheen.)

Chapter 44 Fun With Girlfriend Parties

The more the merrier, I say. I love to have big parties – couples or girlfriends. Frankly, I prefer the girlfriends, especially when Hubby is working or out of town.

To thank my main book supporters I had a fun pot-luck dinner party with wine and soft drinks for fourteen girlfriends. After we chatted, ate, chatted and sipped some more, we watched "Brides Maids" on Hubby's wide-screen television.

Did you know that market research has shown that if you ask people to help with a meal by bringing food or drinks to your party they actually enjoy it more? True. It also helps the hostess emotionally, physically and financially! Those of you on a budget, time, and money wise might want to try this plan. To tell the truth I really enjoy NOT cooking!

Since I was very busy doing two or three book signings a week I picked up little small sandwiches from a local grocery deli (roast beef and turkey) as well as carrot cupcakes. The other gals brought salad, a relish tray, potato salad, etc. I love eating food others prepare, don't you?

In our area we have Xfinity TV, which allows us to pull up any movie when it comes out on DVD as well as some older movies. We can also watch current television shows that we might have missed. (Unfortunately, they still contain the commercials.) Since I write or read during the commercials that doesn't bother me. If you can't, like me, or don't plan ahead to tape your favorite TV shows, it is nice to pull them up later.

Hat parties are fun! These are parties where everyone wears a fun hat. It could be a book group, movie, or bridge group and could even include "hat trading." You will want to serve beverages of some kind. These could be colas, iced tea, maybe wine, or specialty drinks. I feel that if you serve drinks containing alcohol, you need to feed people. We don't want drunk drivers on the road.

Another girlfriend idea might be an overnight P.J. party. It could be a wine tasting party with cheese, crackers or bread and later a yummy casserole. (Check out Fun with Food chapters in my other book.)

Regardless of the kind of girlfriend party you have, if you invite fun girls, plan a fun activity, you and your guests will have an amazing time. I do suggest inviting ten to fifteen. Any more than fifteen guests at my current house becomes a stand-up party.

Plan to do as much of the cleaning, prep, centerpiece, etc., ahead of time. To really enjoy your party don't wait until the last minute to get things done. I know from experience that doing that will wear you out and may make you a tired hostess. If you are relaxed and having fun, your guests will too. If you drink too much you may not be projecting the best of images. Try not to be nervous or anxious about your party.
People will love and appreciate you for having it.

About the worst thing that can happen is if you have a Mary Tyler Moore party, you know, like the ones she had on TV years ago. You invite people and they say they will try to come but don't. I have lived through a couple of these. Both of these parties evolved around dog shows. One of my friends wanted to have an "after dog show" evening dinner. She printed up cute computer invitations along with directions to her home. My friend fixed some of the food and I brought some of my "vein clogging" chocolate iced brownies. We ordered bar-b-que, beans and cole slaw, according to how many we thought were coming. We purchased enough food for thirty people, because some of our friends are big eaters. The party was scheduled for after the last show at dinner time. People were tired and packing up to get out early the next morning. They just didn't want to drive the distance from the show to her house, so we ended up with a "Mary Tyler Moore party" with less than a dozen. But, hey, we had plenty to eat and she and I may have drunk a little bit more than usual.
But we all had fun! She and I sure had plenty of leftovers.

P.S. I just read a party planning article in a magazine that says to plan and make your food a day early and, if you can, plan your outfit ahead of time. The article suggested you stay at home the day of your party. Sounds good to me. Hey – don't know about you but three people make a party for me.

Chapter 45 *Fun Car Shopping With Hubby*

My Hubby is a very bright guy married to a questionably somewhat, sometimes sort of smart-ass gal. He has been my "rock" for all the years we have been married. I appreciate his intelligence, reliability and how caring he is but probably most of all I appreciate his humor. I also love, love his always cute grin. FYI, I'll do about anything to see it!

We were married July 6, 1958. People that know how different we are sometimes wonder how we have managed to stay together for so long. Actually, we wonder that too! However, we love and respect one another. We took our marriage vows seriously and at the end of the day we don't go to bed mad.

After all these years together we usually know what the other one is thinking. However, fall of 2016 I was in for a real surprise. Hubby was having trouble with his ten-year-old Buick. He decided it was time for a newer vehicle. (I had after thirteen years replaced my Ford Mercury Villager with a new Ford Escape in late 2015.) I researched cars for months. I drove all kinds of cars as I figured this would be my last vehicle. This is why Hubby's action was so surprising to me. Since he had gotten his last car new, I was surprised he was going to look at previously owned cars.

Our eldest son and his wife each bought a used Lexus both with over one hundred thousand miles. They have been very pleased. S.C. drives about sixty miles one way to work every day. He is a very smart self-educated mechanical engineer. He was selling his car that had over three thousand miles on it; he felt it would start requiring major repairs. He was able to get a much newer, nicer four-door from their neighbor. He knew its history. I guess this is the reason Hubby wanted to look at a Lexus. He said he didn't want to spend a fortune for a new one. We went to Jacksonville where he was shown three. (Hubby never got into any.) He saw the mileage and the price and said he wasn't interested.

On our way home we had to stop at a fire station to get water after the radiator light went on. During the next two weeks Hubby had to put fluids in it before driving it. We went to a local, well-respected car lot. At this point he said, out of the blue, that he wanted a convertible. Surprise, surprise, surprise! We saw a beautiful Nissan convertible. It was a very attractive off-white with what looked like hand-stitched luggage tan upholstery with a black top. Hubby again did not drive any of the cars. He also mentioned that he thought it was too expensive. Finally, Hubby contacted our youngest son, T.J. In my opinion, he is an internet informational car genius.

Soon we were on our way to Jacksonville as Hubby asked me to go with him to see a car T.J found. I never have driven his car because I like my vehicle. I really didn't care what car he would get as I figured it would take a while for him to make up his mind. (You will soon see how little I knew.) We drove about sixty miles. These days I get very nervous when he is driving so I should have taken a few homeopathic Calm tabs. I avoid driving with him except for on the island. I think he is better on the highway but I just can't relax. We finally arrived at the Chevrolet dealer. There in front were a Corvette and a Camaro – both painted very acid yellow. The petite, professional black sales gal was there for my husband's appointment. She said she would get in the back so I could sit in front with my husband. "Oh, no, that's fine, if he decides that he is serious about it I'll take it out later." I had to giggle to myself as these two "unlikely together people" drove off.

When they returned, surprise, surprise, surprise, he wanted me to drive it. I did and when I started to see if it had any pick-up I found it coming up short compared to my Escape. Just in time I saw a cop. I returned and Hubby asked me what I thought. I told him the car wasn't for me so it didn't make any difference. After looking it over I asked Hubby if he really wanted it. He said he did. I was in shock. It was not the sleek Lexus I thought he had in my mind. It is a bit wider and longer with wide doors and lower than what we were used to. However, it looked like new with new tires and low mileage. We talked a minute and I realized that he wanted it. I offered two thousand dollars less than what the dealer was asking, which according to our son was extremely well priced. She said, "I don't think they will take that." I said, "Please ask, okay?" She disappeared and out came "Bubba," not his real name, but you get the picture. He started to give his pitch to Hubby. I told him he had to deal with me. (I'm the one who has worked in sales and not easily intimidated.) Hubby needed me to work the deal as he is way too sweet and nice. Bubba said, "Let me tell you what I do here." I quickly said, "I don't care what you do here – all I care about is that my Hubby seems to think he wants it, and we've made you a fair offer." Bubba then showed us an ad for the upcoming Thanksgiving weekend. The dealerships planned to "special" it for four or five thousand dollars more than their current price. I said, "That makes perfect sense being that this car was for sale in Boca for five months, then in Knoxville for three or four months and you have had it for sale for almost three months. It sure makes sense to raise the price." I went on to tell him, "We don't have to buy this car. We can go down to the light, turn right where there are several other dealerships.

You have an interested buyer, right here, right now who has made you an offer. Show us you are ready to deal." He seemed to be in shock. He said, "About the very best we could do would be to take another thousand off." I said, "Hubby, would that work for you?" He said it would.

The paperwork was passed on to another salesperson who wanted to sell us an extended warranty, etc. He said to me, "Are you excited about your new car?" I said, "Not me." "Why?" he asked. "It's not a Porsche Boxster." Driving home I noticed how noisy it was and told Hubby, "I'm not taking road trips in this thing." It wasn't very comfortable either. I told Hubby if women suddenly start coming onto him it could be because they like his car. Don't think about having an affair because my girlfriends and I can easily track the "yellow bird." He grinned. I asked him why he wanted it and he told me he couldn't think of any reason NOT to get it. The car is in great condition with brand-new tires – no scratches, dents or dings and the mileage was just a little over twenty thousand miles with a good warranty. It looks like brand new. It's nice to look at and he seems to enjoy driving it with the top down.

If he is happy, I'm happy. He was especially happy to get an extra one thousand dollars off. We have had it about six months and I still haven't driven it, nor do I really want to, but if he is happy, I'm happy.

My hubby is a guy who I thought I really knew; however, I have been in shock for several months. I just don't understand how a person can go from wanting a sleek Lexus to a Camaro (which I think is so opposite.) I also don't understand Hubby making his decision after driving one car. Hubby has been very predicable all our married life. He would come home from work at the same time every day He never varied his taste in clothes, etc. What can I say – he shook this old bitch up. I will say he seems to be having fun driving it but he often asks me to drive my vehicle when he thinks we'll encounter narrow parking spaces. The doors on the Camaro are so wide and it is so low and so a bit difficult for us to get out of. However, Hubby loves driving with the top down – good for him.

With my allergies I don't do that.

What I am really glad about is the bright yellow color because it makes people see him and get out of his way. All good!

Chapter 46 Fun With Queen Nonna

This chapter was written by my oldest son S.C. Hoover.

It all started when I moved to Metter, Georgia. Metter is an archetypical small southern town. It has a downtown wrapped around a rectangular park. There is a courthouse, a diner, several barbershops, antique stores, and a pawn shop, a couple of banks, a dollar store, the Georgia Power office and a hardware store facing the park. There are several churches within a block of the square including both kinds of Baptist. Residential streets run off the square north and south. Medians in the streets are planted with Azaleas and Dogwoods. Population is about three thousand in the city and nine thousand in Candler County.

The prospect of small-town life always intrigued me. I grew up in suburban Atlanta, and then moved outside of Cleveland, Ohio. Finding a job that allows one to earn a living was the hard part. In 2000 the company I work for set up a factory in a town near Metter. I got the opportunity to move away from snowy northern Ohio, back to Georgia, and Metter. As their motto says, "Everything is better in Metter." Elyria, Ohio, wasn't bad in the summer, but overall Metter was better. My wife at the time and I purchased a house on Kennedy Street, four blocks off the square. A nice three bedroom brick house on a corner. Azaleas, camellias, other flowering shrubs and several pecan trees graced the lush green yard. Metter has everything you really need close at hand. The grocery store, bank, hardware store, post office and fried chicken take-out were all within a short bicycle ride. Not far away, Statesboro has a mall, Movie Theater, restaurants and big box stores. After about six thirty in the evening, sitting on my screened-in front porch you could count the cars that went by on one hand.

When my wife and I moved to Metter we had been dog less for about six months. At the time, Metter did not have any kind of leash law. Many people allowed their dogs to roam at large. One dog that would come by our house as part of her daily rounds was a beautiful little adolescent mix breed that looked like a three-quarter-scale Golden Retriever. Based on her spotted tongue, maybe a Cocker/Chow mix. Somehow we decided we wanted her, although my wife and I forever debated on which of us wanted her first, and "whose dog" she was. We learned that she was being loosely cared for by a couple who lived a few blocks away, and that we could have her. She was being called Tracy by the couple but we called her Trixie. Later when we were walking her, some young girls came running up exclaiming "Guinevere"! Turns out they were another stop on Trixie, Tracy, Guinevere's daily rounds.

Sometime in our first few months in Metter we became acquainted with the dog-catcher. A scrounge-looking pit bull came into our yard with a large tranquilizer dart hanging off its side. We were able to catch the dog and remove the dart without much problem. We called Animal Control to come and get him. They had tried and failed to catch the dog previously, even to the extent of darting him. From this encounter the dog-catcher learned we were dog people.

Several weeks later a dog we had never seen before showed up at our house. She was a young adult mixed breed. Her body and markings were similar to a Border Collie, but with a more blocky-shaped head with a broad muzzle. A bit more elongated, but a head that looked like she might have some Rottweiler or, more likely in Metter, Pit in her bloodline. She actually looked a lot like a Bernese Mountain Dog. She has a very sweet disposition and an air of intelligence in her almost apelike brown eyes. My stepdaughter suggested we name her Nonna, after the Border Collie in Peter Pan. She quickly won our hearts. One of the "cute" characteristics she would do was the trick of giving you a nip to get your attention. This is a common trick among Collies. Just a quick pinch, pinch, pinch with her front teeth usually on the back of your thigh. She would tune the nip to your personal pain tolerance. After a few times, I started swatting her back, and for me she turned it down to at least a light nibble. At first it was quite startling and a little painful. She obviously thought it quite hilarious to see humans jump out of their shoes, and scream when she caught them by surprise. Other than that she was great around humans, dogs and cats. We kept an eye on her around small children, but she never attempted it with a child.

A month or so later the dog-catcher stopped by in passing, seeing Nonna out in the carport with my ex. He asked about Nonna, basically wanting to know how she was working out. In the course of the conversation it became apparent the dogcatcher had dropped her off in our yard. He admitted to doing the same thing successfully with a few other good dogs he didn't want to see put down. If it didn't work out, or someone called in a complaint on the dog, worst come to worst he would just go and pick it back up. He was working as the county animal control officer because he loved animals. His placement strategy was a little unconventional, but pretty effective, at least in our case.

Nonna became the dog queen of Metter. We would walk the two dogs to the ball fields and Nature Park several times a week. Every time at least a few of the neighborhood dogs would tag along. Among regulars was Shadow, a large white neutered male German Shepherd, and Petey, a female black lab mix. The pack of dogs would have a great time running up and down the creek and chasing each other in the open grassy areas. There was always at least one or two extra dogs. Depending on the route, it might be a different mix. For fun, one time I took a long non-direct circuitous route and wound up with a total of twelve! The dogs all got along, but it was obvious that Nonna was alpha.

One day we were walking down a street, and this guy in a yard stopped me to warn that I shouldn't come down that street, as his dog was vicious with other dogs and had "tore up a couple." Apparently "Coco" had a reputation Just as we were talking, a snarling Chocolate Lab came charging out of the garage after Nonna. There was fifteen seconds of snarling, swirling, snapping and flying dog spit. You have to be very careful breaking up a dog fight. We tried, but it is very easy to get bit and it was over very quickly. Coco ended up on her back, with Nonna on top. Nonna had her in complete submission with her throat exposed. I pulled Nonna off, and Coco ran back home, yelping with her tail tucked. No injury to either dog, but Coco now knew who was queen.

A few weeks later Coco saw Trixie from one-half a block away and came charging over, teeth bared and hair up. Nonna was bringing up the rear and out of sight at first. When Coco saw her at the last instant, she made a quick about-face and departed at high speed, yelping with her tail tucked.

A typical cowardly bully.

On another occasion, we were walking through the neighborhood and I noticed some guys looking around a vacant lot. A truck lettered with the name of a local tree service company was pulled up in the pine straw. Apparently, they were going to cut some trees prior to a house being built and were checking out the job. Now, don't get me wrong, tree cutting is an honorable job. But it is hard dirty work and more than a few that do that work are a bit rough. They may very well clean up well, but this group in particular was a tough looking bunch of rednecks. I wasn't paying much attention to what the dogs were doing, when all of a sudden the biggest, baddest nastiest guy of all was cussing, and picked up a large stick and was chasing after Nonna. I said, "Hey, hey, what's going on? Don't hit my dog." The gentleman then said, "That goddamned dog tried to take a chunk out of my ass!" I said," That can't be. She's not like that." I wasn't thinking of her clever little Collie dog nipping trick. One of the other guys said, "Mister, I don't know who you are, but I saw her, and if I were you I would keep on walking." I called the dogs and exited stage right. Later it hit me what she had done. Nonna humor at its best.

Walking a different direction down toward the county pond, was a house with seven or eight small to medium-sized dogs. Seemed like fifteen. Whenever anyone went by they would charge out, yapping and raising hell. Safety in numbers. Trixie would detour a block over to go around and avoid them. One time in particular, I went by and they came out. Nonna was behind me. She just strolled along, apparently ignoring them, sniffing here and there. Meanwhile, I was calling her to come on and get past, which she also ignored. Casually she sniffed her way along to their yard, squatted, and peed. The dogs were now barking furiously, slowly advancing. Nonna looked up as if she had just noticed their presence. She then barked deep and loud, "WOOF, WOOF"! All of them immediately quit yapping, and carefully slinked back into the back yard.

We had had Nonna about seven years when my wife and I divorced. Being fully grown when we first got her, Nonna must have been at least nine at that point, and still in prime shape. Believe it or not, we agreed to joint custody of the dogs when we split. My ex moved just a few blocks away. I would keep them most of the time, but she would come walk them while I was at work, and sometimes keep them on the weekend.

After a year or so, I met Becky at a big box store in Statesboro. I was going to buy a towel bar, and she was coming out with bags of mulch. I helped load the mulch in her Z4 roadster and got her phone number.
Turned out she had also recently divorced.

We hit it off and quickly became steadies. When I began spending time at Becky's house many times the dogs would go with me. Becky lived in a house overlooking an eighty-acre lake. Nonna, in particular, really liked the place, running deer in the woods and wading in the water. Often she would lie on the back porch looking out over the lake. Nonna and Becky also hit it off. Becky had Nonna's seal of approval as they quickly bonded.   At one point while Becky and I were dating, the two dogs in joint custody grew into three. My ex had picked up a third stray on a walk. It was a Golden Doodle. Her "plan" was to find it a home. She suggested I find somebody at work to take him. I suggested getting him a dog tag with "Your Name Here." Anyway, his name became "Happy." I tried changing it to "Tiger," but it didn't stick. Happy was and is a clown. Very vocal and eager to please. He loves to go get muddy and then climb in your lap.   A couple of years went by, and Becky and I were married. I moved from Metter into Becky's house by the lake. Enough was enough with the joint custody thing. My ex took Trixie. Becky and I took Nonna and Happy.   One day I took the dogs with me to Metter to do some work on my old house we were now renting. A neighborhood boy came by, and said, "Hey, that looks like my Grandma's dog," indicating Happy. I said that maybe it is, and why don't you take him to her and see. He went off with Happy on a leash, and came back twenty minutes later. "Yeah, it's hers." "Why did you bring him back?" "She said she don't need no damn dog." Well, okay, mystery solved. I heard later she not only got another dog, but it had a litter of puppies.

Nonna was now queen of Brannen Lake. There was a Husky down the street that was aggressive with other male dogs. One day Chance came into our yard, and jumped Happy. Nonna rushed to the rescue. Just like Coco years before, Nonna instantly put him on his back and into submission. When Nonna let him up he went straight home. Once again, lots of dog spit, but no blood. All other dogs in the neighborhood gave Nonna her due respect and allowed her safe and unimpeded transit through their yards.

Not so much with Happy.

Besides the nip thing, there was only one thing Nonna did bad. I hate to use the "D" word, but it's true. Nonna was a digger. Usually she liked to dig depressions behind shrubbery. She liked the shade and the cool earth on her belly. Becky was worried about the bushes and periodically I would fill the holes back in, and try and dissuade her. At one point she decided to create a major earthwork right in the middle of Becky's beautifully manicured back yard. She constructed a twelve-foot-diameter circular trench, with a branch coming off of it. From above it looked like a large Q. She would lay in the grass patch in the middle, survey her domain. Gazing out across the lake. If you looked on Google Earth, you literally could see it from space.

It was a test of wills. I would scold her, and fill it up, and she would dig it back out. I made several trips to get more bags of top soil and grass seed. I think in the end I gave up, and then she let me have my way. I didn't bother her about the dens behind the bushes anymore.

In the heat of July 2014 when she must have been at least fifteen or sixteen, we came home and she was gone. We searched the area for several days, talked to people who had seen her and posted signs. One person had seen her coming out of a pond several miles away. Another person saw her heading up a dirt road. A couple days later we got a call. Someone who had seen the sign, saw a posting on Facebook from somebody who had found a dog that looked like Nonna. She had wandered into the yard of a vet tech.

She was severely dehydrated, tick infested, had a cut on her right front leg and was exhausted. She was at least five miles back in the other direction from where she had been sighted two days before. After a trip to the vet, an IV and some antibiotics she did recover, but not to the same level of robustness.

Over the next few years Nonna started to show signs of aging. Cataracts started forming in her eyes, she lost some weight, bloodwork indicated kidney problems and her hearing started going.

Then as time went on she continued to decline. She became nearly blind and deaf, she lost muscle tone and developed a cough that I know was congestive heart failure. Even so, she continued to eat well and still go across the street into the wood to do her business as usual. Most days she would cool off with a dip in the lake. Typically when I came home, she would be standing in the front yard with her legs and belly wet. Also, as she always had, she continued to have very active dreams. You could see and hear her running and barking in her sleep. Dogs spend a lot of time sleeping and dreaming. I always wondered what Nonna's dream world was like. Had she aged in the dream world?

At this point she had been part of my life for sixteen years. She had to be eighteen or more. We knew she was failing and hoped she would go peacefully in her sleep one night. It wasn't to be. Finally she had declined to where she couldn't get out the dog door or walk across the hardwood floor without her back legs splaying out from under her. After hearing her lose control and fall trying to get out the dog door late one night, I got up and carried her outside; she could only walk ten or fifteen feet at a time. At one point she laid down right where her earthwork had been. I had decided that's where we should bury her. I thought about getting the gun at that point. I really didn't want her dying on an examination table at the vet's office. Previously at the vet, they had muzzled her when she got her shots. It wasn't her favorite place. I thought putting her down myself at home would be the right thing to do. Nevertheless, I could not bring myself to do it.

Instead, the next morning I carried her out to the car, and we took her to the vet. I felt a bit guilty, both for initiating the act, then paying someone else to do the job. It was a very sad ride to Metter. We waited outside in the car with the air conditioning running until the doctor was ready. I carried her in and laid her on the examination table. At least they didn't muzzle her. The vet and his assistant were very gentle and empathetic. Nonna seemed relaxed. The vet administered the injection in her left front leg. She closed her eyes, and less than a minute her heart stopped. Trying not to cry too much, I picked up the now limp, but still warm body in my arms and put it in the back seat of the car. We took her body home. I dug a hole right where she had laid down the night before, right where she once looked over her domain. I got on my knees and leaned down to gently place the body in the bottom of the hole with her head facing toward the lake. I adjusted her head, legs and tail. After one last look I started shoveling dirt on top of the body. I started at her hind quarters and moved forward. Soon only her head was showing through the loose dirt. A few more shovels and she disappeared beneath the earth. I finished filling the hole and piled up the extra dirt in a mound over the grave.

I hadn't expected to be so impacted, but I felt gutted. It was Monday and I had planned to go to work. I went up the back steps, propped the shovel on the back porch, took off my gloves and put them on the outdoor bar. I went inside, got a beer out of the fridge, sat down and drank it. I wasn't going to work that day.

Chapter 47 *Fun Being the Star of Your Own Life*

My daughter-in-law is absolutely amazing! She's a great wife to my eldest son.

She studied to be an accountant and was successful in that field. She then decided to go into banking and became a vice president of the bank. During that time she started a part-time catering business which she later developed into a fulltime successful business. She sold it, moved to another state and now owns another successful business that employs at least a half-dozen people. Plus, get this, she is as beautiful on the inside as she is on the outside. She is what people call a good soul. FYI – Her father was a minister as is her brother. (I knew my son really loved her when he started going to church again.) At Christmas time she and our eldest son brought a sweet potato soufflé, a seven-layer salad, rolls, a standing rib roast and two wonderful tenderloins PLUS the most awesome gorgeous five-layer wonderful carrot cake. I've heard the way to a man's heart is through his stomach. (Certainly a way to this mother-in-law's heart.) Maybe it wasn't a bad idea to say, "I hate to cook." I don't think I'm a horrible cook but, honey, she is a ten! Or is that a twenty? Is she a star? I say yes, yes, yes!!! But what do I know? Be the star of your own life. Keep learning – no matter what your age. (I had an uncle who graduated from college at fifty.)

It only takes thirty seconds for someone to form an impression. Try to always look your best, especially at work. Are you ready for that surprise meeting with your boss? Even though your family and friends adore you (most of the time), people at work may not. Put your best foot forward, always trying to remember to respect others and their ideas. You need to work to get them to respect and appreciate you. Be kind to all people from the cleaning personnel to the CEO. Remember, people you work with don't have to like you. (Treat that server nicely too, please.) Have I always? Maybe not, but the older I get the more important it seems to be.

Making a presentation? Make it an opportunity for advancement. If you haven't had a lot of experience, practice with a friend or better yet, have them take a video of your presentation. After a trip to the restroom, take a deep breath and ask God for guidance. Look professional. Wear garments that are made from good quality fabric. Make sure your clothes fit well. Unless you're in a very creative field – make it conservative. (Think evening television anchor.) Guys, if you are low on funds and need a suit or jacket, check out Goodwill. Good grooming is oh so important, too! If you have tattoos – hide them with clothing, as they are very distracting. Although I have gotten used to them, there are many people who feel they have a lower-class look. (Sorry, but that's the truth.) I agree that more people are seeing tattoos as a personal art expression. Or – you got drunk and went crazy. Tattoos can be removed. Some celebrities are doing this now. If you want to progress upward, you need to (if you haven't already) take a Dale Carnegie course or go to your local community college and take public speaking. Read and study the self-improvement books or better yet listen to CDs while driving, but only if you can do this safely. DON'T TEXT AND DRIVE or you could be TEXTING AND DYING. You could kill someone else, perhaps small children. (I would not want to live with that guilt.)

Make your presentations bright, meaningful and positive. Consider what objections you might encounter and think through what you would say. Do not, I repeat, DO NOT take negative comments personally. It isn't about you – this is business!!!

Don't let them "see you cry." Hopefully, not even in the restroom; you are on your way to being a star, remember? Maybe this is one of your life lessons and will be one of your top learning opportunities. Whatever happens in life, ask yourself what's God wanting you to learn?

Keep in mind the Boy Scout motto, "Be prepared"; over prepared is even better.

One way of being prepared is never getting yourself involved emotionally or sexually with your boss or bosses.

Keep your personal problems private.

Don't babysit for your boss. If asked say, "I'm so sorry but I already have plans," or "I'm so sorry but I'm committed to a family birthday." It's okay.

I'm sure God will forgive you if it is a little white lie.

To become and stay a star, don't forget that even stars get tired and irritable. For heaven's sake – take your vacations. Take care of your mind and body! Use your sunscreen, don't drink too much or, if you go to Colorado, don't do too much pot. Come back to work rested and relaxed and hopefully not to a lot of credit card debt. PLAN AHEAD.

Remember my slogan, "Hope and pray for the best for all concerned, but remember to cover your ass and assets." Even movie stars have lost all their money due to poor financial management. Don't be like that. Save for a rainy day. If necessary you need to be able to go six months without income.

To save money, pick up a bag of salad and some microwave meals if you don't have time to fix a proper meal. Life is not always doing what you WANT to do, it is about planning and THINKING ahead. According to experts, preparing and eating food at home is the number one way to save money and calories. Be the star of your own life. (I find if I avoid shopping with girlfriends or from catalogs I don't spend as much.)

P.S. Think ahead, and plan ahead to get ahead. You can do it!

Chapter 48 Fun With Food Fitness and Foolish Behavior

Can you imagine, a doctor once asked me if I lacked appetite? (At the time I was about twenty-five pounds overweight.) I answered, "Looking at me do you really think that has happened?" He grinned. (Don't mess with me, mister, doctor or not.) I was thin when I was born. I was slender until I was about twelve. Then I grew tall and began to get curves. The first year in college I put on about twenty pounds. I lost about fifteen the next summer.

From that point on in life, I had to be more careful of what I ate.

I didn't have to really diet until I was pregnant. My doctor threatened to put me in the hospital if I gained more than twenty pounds. I would sit and cry at lunch before eating a piece of bologna, a glass of chocolate milk and two slices of tomato. It was horrible.

I did my exercises and soon was back to my normal weight after having my eldest. Three years later, PG again. Another doctor talked about my weight getting over twenty pounds. I came home from the hospital only one pound overweight. In the fifties the doctors really thought it wasn't healthy to gain over twenty pounds. From that time on I have struggled. I really had no problem as long as I was showing my Dalmatians. Once I reached sixty and was having knee problems, I stopped going in the ring and the pounds came on. Hubby and I had three moves in about five years. I don't do well with the stress of moving. I need energy, so I eat. Unfortunately, soon I was thirty-five pounds overweight. Ugh, ugh, UGH!!!

Through the years I have gone to Weight Watchers three times and to TOPS (Take Off Pounds Successfully). My Mayo orthopedic doctor told me to lose weight and to get into an exercise program. I went to Curves for about seven years until they closed in both my Florida and North Carolina hometowns. I lost about twenty pounds and my knee was doing fine. Curves closed and I was writing my Panties book and not getting exercise. After the book came out, one evening I got up out of my chair and heard my left knee pop. I had torn my meniscus. A day or two later my Hubby was in the hospital with a very scary intestinal problem. Several days later, he had surgery. The doctor untwisted his intestine but recommended another surgery two months later – successful, thank God. During that time I had two cortisone shots, which helped some. I put off surgery for six months. After surgery it took six months before I was back to normal or in my case, better than normal. My weight has been the same for about five or six years, but I still NEED to lose twenty pounds.

What to do, what to do?

I went to Zumba with a thirty-one-year-old girlfriend (once). The following week she was in a car accident. The week after that I over-extended my shoulder. Crap! Sometimes it isn't easy being me.

Oprah knows a lot! Hey, she wrote an entire book about what she knows. What this old bitch (me) knows is food and fitness under the right conditions can be fun. I also know that if you aren't wise on the kind and amount of food you eat, you will gain weight. And if you want to lose weight, you need to exercise, too! Damn, damn, damn!!! Yes, Oprah, we know you struggle too. But maybe you have a personal chef and trainer? At least we don't have to make "appearances" like you do, thank God.

I know for sure, excuses don't get it done. We have to step up and take care of the gift God gave us. May God help us all! It is time to make hard decisions and just do it! P.S. Zumba or Jazzercise, anyone?

P.P.S. Now I plan to go to Tai Chi, which looks so easy, but it is so hard. Incredibly, you can actually feel your abs working. I am also looking for an old-bitch slower Zumba class.

Chapter 49 *Fun Being Happy or Unhappy*

Unconsciously, I truly believe that some people do everything possible to make themselves unhappy or depressed.

I have a couple of younger friends who sometimes tell me they are depressed. I ask them how much sugar they have had. (I know sugar can depress me.)

In a roundabout way I ask them what they are doing to help others. (Studies have shown that those who volunteer by helping others are happier and live longer lives.) I also ask them what they are doing with their friends.

Experts say social interaction helps too.

How to be happier? This is what I learned, life is what you make it. Yeah, sure, you say you don't have my life. Of course not, however, if you read every chapter in this book you will find out about some of the crappy things that have happened to me. You have to "dust yourself off" and go on, kiddo.

And yes, it often isn't easy or fun.

For you younger gals the best advice I can give you is to get as much education as you can. Avoid getting pregnant and wait, wait, wait until you are thirty or close to it before getting married. Why? Because you'll be much more likely to succeed in your marriage and as a parent.

Remember this true fact. Guys can't walk at three months and their brains aren't mature (if a guy's brains are ever mature) until they are twenty-six to twenty-seven. I have two adult sons and an adult grandson, so I can speak from watching how slow they matured. Both sons married young, both divorced, unfortunately, and are now "thank God" both remarried and very happy. Grandson hopefully got it right by waiting until he was thirty-one. Granddaughter-in-love, as I like to say, was twenty-eight. They both had several long-term not-great relationships that made them really appreciate each other. They both came from loving families with similar values, similar religions and with loving supportive long-time married parents and grandparents with long, good marriages. (We all love them and try to keep in close touch. Hopefully they will make wise career and money decisions.) The single most important decision for you to remember is marrying the right person. I know of many middle-age and older women that are living a life full of struggles because of marrying the wrong man. In most cases Mom and Dad tried to talk them out of marriage to "their man," the parent telling them, "You marry him and you can't come home again." Years later one daughter, divorced, kids raised, was asked to move back home to help care for Dad and Mom while holding down a full-time job. Due to the economy she lost her job. Now, after Dad's death, Mom is "supercritical" and "very difficult." Daughter is working several part-time jobs, has no insurance and is fast closing in on sixty. Did I mention severe back problems? In spite of all this, she is generally a fun, positive person.

Another gal I know, who is in her fifties, married young at twenty-six or so, divorced a year later after her husband became abusive. Thank goodness she divorced him and there were no kids. She is a successful professional. She'll probably never find true happiness. Sad to say, she seems to dwell on all bad things that have happened to her. She takes no responsibilities for her actions, which in most cases, causes the disasters. Everything is always someone else's fault. She is the youngest child. Her parents divorced when she was very young. Her mother caught Dad with another woman. He didn't want a divorce but she wouldn't forgive him, so he moved his successful business to another state. He told his kids, "You can stay with your mom and have nothing, or come with me." The little girl chose Mom who worked several jobs just to put food on the table. Dad turned into a real loser. (In my opinion.) He ended up with several more wives, kids and penniless. What he did to this daughter, in my opinion, really messed her up. She always feels a guy is not going to commit and stay. Guess what? They don't. What part he has in her enjoying being a victim – I don't know. Could she be happy? Yes, if she would admit she has some problems, get some professional help and maybe be not quite so self-absorbed. Life is not all about us regardless of what we think. I feel sorry for her but at some point we each need to step up to the plate and try to grow up. You can't if you don't accept responsibility for your actions. But what do I know? If she volunteered and helped others she would help herself.

What if you grew up in a really bad situation? Mom dies, Dad remarries a real bad b _ _ _ _. Stepmom beats her. Dad, the drunk, makes her buy her own clothes at ten out of her babysitting money and beats on her too. She marries at seventeen and is a mother a year later. He has a drinking problem too, and is soon running around. She has another child. She stayed with him until the children were out of high

177

school. She worked her way from a clerk to manager of a large drugstore. My friend bought a nice condo and had some fun. She remarried and after this new husband took everything of value and sold it, she divorced him. Years later my friend found a wonderful man who loved and appreciated her. They sold her place, bought a truck and travel trailer and traveled all over the USA. Now she is a widow, has limited funds and serious health issues. She has income from Social Security, a small G.I. widow's fund plus a little extra from painting and selling her art. This gal is a lot of fun. She attends church often and volunteers at a food shelter. She counts her blessings, and two of them are her loving adult children.

Remember, it is not where and how you start out in life. It is how and what you do to better yourself. It is how you use your God-given talents. It helps to be grateful to God, and ask him to guide you on your journey. What happiness isn't, is spending all your time making money to pay off purchases you don't need. There is a BIG difference between want and real need. The sooner you figure this out, the happier you will be. Choose your friends and your life partner carefully – they reflect what you think of yourself.

Life isn't always easy. This makes being happy more difficult sometimes. What to do? When negative situations happen to you, in order not to get depressed, you need to look for any and all positives. For instance, a good friend who cares, someone who smiles at you, even blue skies, sunshine, gentle rain and those sweet colorful blooms popping up through the snow.

Throughout my long life I have known people who see the glass half empty and those who see it half full. Guess what? You can be either. The choice is yours. If depression runs in your family, you can still be an upbeat personality if you want to. A half full or empty wine glass clearly needs more wine. If you get depressed easily for no reason, look at your diet. It could be as simple as eliminating sugar and reducing your caffeine. I'm not sure who said "You are what you eat," but I believe that to be true.

If you are dealing with a lot in life – be smart and seek professional help. If you can't afford to go to a psychiatrist or psychologist, perhaps a high school counselor or a member of the clergy could help you.

Someone I saw on television wrote a book about happiness. She said fifty to sixty percent of our genetic makeup determines if we are basically happy or not. She also said that if a student watches a happy video before a test they get higher scores. Very interesting, don't you think?

From my many self-improvement books, I learned the main secret to life is finding things for which to be grateful, then thank God, or the universe for these blessings. Things like a beautiful sunrise, sunset, a hug, a smile, a summer breeze, soft rain and all the things we can sometimes take for granted. As most of you may know, I believe in asking God for guidance. Just pausing to ask for daily direction and taking in deep breaths certainly helps me.

It is important to forgive and if at all possible, forget bad things said or done to us. Look at Oprah and what she overcame and what good she continues to do for others. Have you watched her show? If I had lots of money I would send all my friends the "Oprah" magazine. She is one very bright woman who has shared a lot of what she has learned with others. You might want to buy her new book, *What I Know for Sure*.

Another element in gaining and keeping happiness is to have close friends who support you. I have learned that some of my very best friends seem to, without knowing it, drain my energy. Thus, I have backed away from these gals by not communicating as frequently. I still love them but I value my mental health. It is difficult to hear the same negative stuff over and over. (Sometimes stuff from relationships long ago.) It is one thing helping a friend, another enabling them, don't you agree?

Other things that make me happy are the colors I surround myself with and the ones I wear. Even though I love wearing black I wear it with bright accents or colorful scarves or tops. Other things that will help you to be happy are getting a good night's sleep and eating three healthy, regularly timed meals that avoid sugar, bread and white potatoes. We all like fast food but I know I feel better and happier when I don't have it.

A pet will help you, too. It is difficult not to smile at some of the things they do. I've had cats and dogs, but dogs seem to "get me" more. I adore Dalmatian puppies but I am past the age for all the hard work involved in their care.

I enjoy Diva, my older Dalmatian. She still runs at racetrack speed across our yard. I can't help but smile and praise her. She is so funny when it is getting near her afternoon five fifteen feeding time. She tries staring me down, sitting in front of me sending mental messages. If I am writing, she puts her head on my knee or on the arm of my chair and keeps looking at me. If I look at her she starts sticking her tongue in and out. Sometimes she is very patient if I am on the phone. If it gets to be six o'clock she starts the knee thing again. She is wonderful, not like some of my former Dals that would get vocal and try to talk to me, slowly working up to a bark. Diva has a wonderful bladder, thank God. (Hubby and I give her ample opportunities to go out.) Diva is the perfect alarm dog as she never barks unless the doorbell rings. She sounds like she will tear the person apart.

Once I start chatting with them, she thinks they have come to see her. She always remembers her fans. Not all Dals are as sweet or as easy as she is. Dals are not for everyone. If they weren't so pretty, fun and sweet, you may want to kill them the first couple of years. Diva brings us a great deal of joy and happiness.

Someone said joy is long-term, happiness is considered short-term. I read somewhere that "happiness" is a lack of sadness. Something I try to remember.

Music, especially calming, classical music like Mozart or Debussy brings happiness. I am not a fan of Brahms or Bach. To me they contain negative, soulful notes that are depressing! Listen to music that makes you happy if you can. Some people I know seem to only be happy when they are spending money. No kidding, they can't seem to go into a store and not buy anything. Or they go overboard on home improvements. Granted, these improvements look nice, but I wouldn't do them. Yes, we do spend money keeping our property up. There is a difference. Ask yourself if you are going to get your money back if you were to sell your property tomorrow. We have neighbors who don't seem to understand. They have added onto their house, put in a very expensive pool, re-done the entire inside and outside of their home. Yet complain at our own homeowners meetings about houses in our community going for less than what people have invested. They don't seem to understand: 1. The economy changes. 2. That their expensive personal choices might not be what the next person is willing to pay top dollar for. 3. The difference between up-keep and over-the-top improvements. 4. Some investments don't ever pay off.

If you have the money to pay for these improvements and don't mind losing that money, and don't have to put these expenses on a credit card, then who am I to tell you not to do it. The problem is, as I see it, that some people get themselves into more and more credit trouble.

I hear of young families buying lots of toys, clothes, etc., for their kids because they didn't have all that stuff growing up. I really feel our educational system is missing the mark by not teaching life skills to our young people. Are kids today taught how to balance a checkbook and how to be accountable? I don't think so. Are they taught how to take up a hem, sew on a button or plan a budget? Are they taught how to plan healthy menus for a week, to buy food economically and prepare their own meals? Don't think so. Have our young people been taught how to keep a home clean? To make a bed? Have they been taught anything important in caring for themselves and the place they will someday live in, or are they like some of the young people I've met, especially teen-age girls, expecting to marry someone who makes big bucks, someone who will take care of them, someone who will provide them with a cook and a maid? Boys who expect to make it big as a singer or movie action star. People should have dreams but, baby, they need a backup plan. The old bitch me, says plan (very, very important) and pray for the best, but, baby cakes, you need to prepare for the worst. You need a minimum of six months to a year pay saved to cover you if you were to lose your job. Or – you could lose everything! Car, apartment, house, credit – everything.

Where would you go and what would you do?

Your happiness depends on how you handle your life. Be responsible and be happy with less material things. Save your money for education to improve yourself.

You can be happy! Ask God to help you make good decisions and remember to thank God for every goodness that comes your way. You can do it!

P.S. Have safe sex. Don't get pregnant until you are in a really good marriage for several years. Plan your life. Don't depend on others for your happiness.

Chapter 50 Fun Getting a Guy to Listen

Can that be – a guy really listening?

According to a study done by Columbia University, most people speak at one hundred words a minute while our brains can process one thousand words a minute. Sometimes people tune out slow speech. The study must have been done on women. Men usually tune us out most of the time regardless of how fast or slow we speak. Right? This is especially true if we are asking our Hubby to actually do something. According to my main source of information, "Women's

World," the way to get a man's attention, is to get right to your point. If you give too much information you lose them. Details are a woman's thing, facts are what a man wants. It might be best to sit or stand next to him. Women like looking at the person speaking, men don't. They find face to face confrontational.

Check out author Kevin Hogan's book, *The Psychology of Persuasion*. According to that book it is a fact men don't like women's high-pitched voices. Higher-pitched sounds like nagging. Interesting fact is that dogs respond better to lower voices too. Higher tones, I hear, cause a man to be "anxious" and less likely to focus on your words. Lower your voice and hopefully you'll both feel better. (Interesting, lowering your voice sounds very similar to a man's, just saying.)

Move closer to your guy as you're talking. This is supposed to help his focus. They say it is biological, as women are programmed to hear someone calling to them, like as a crying child. Men are programmed to focus on what they need to do – now.

All I have to say is – good luck. Sometimes fortune smiles on me and I can get a man to listen. Frankly, it is usually not a relative.

Let it be a challenge to you, as it is to me. Why are women attracted to men? We all like a challenge and a cute smile.

Chapter 51 *Fun at More Dog Shows*

Recently I ran into an adorable young gal who I have seen at dog shows since she was a pre-teen. She was looking as beautiful as I remembered, yet now she is married and has a baby boy. After saying "hi" I said, "Gosh, I thought he would be cuter." Okay, I do sometimes speak without thinking. That's not something you didn't know if you read my first book, right? She laughed – thank God! – I said, "Maybe he'll get lucky and grow up to be really good-looking, like you!" (Hey, I know how to kiss up when I have clearly messed up.) I love to go to dog shows – especially if some of our dogs or those that go back to some of my breeding dogs win. And yes, I love hanging out with fun people.

At the Dalmatian Club of America (DCA) I got to hang out with some of my very favorite people. One of them is Buddy – he is a fun friend of mine from Tampa. (His wife, Cheryl, a

bestie of mine, died four years ago.) Buddy drove to the Ocala, Florida, area from Tampa to hang out with me. (It's a five- to six-hour trip, round trip.) He did this two days in a row. He is so much fun. We love to joke about the competition. Sorry – at least I admit it! I wanted him to see Billy (Ch. Chermar Atlantis Wall Street Billionaire, and his cousin, Ch. American Road Harley Sportster). These two beautiful boys go back to Ch. Star Run Atlantis Red "Clover," a bitch that was bred by Cheryl and Judy Clark. Clover, who went back to my breeding, was a liver (brown and white) that won a big "Best In Sweep" in Tampa before Cheryl showed her to her championship. Clover was invited to the Eukanuba
Invitational Show.

Her grandkids are very nice – one is even an all-breed Best In Show. The other, also a liver, is one of the top winning bitches in our breed. (Bitch means female.)

Buddy is like the fun brother I never had. We talk every week or so. Love him! After years of hearing about Buddy, my Hubby finally got to spend some time with him when he came to stay with us a few days. Some pair. Now Hubby tells me to say "Hi" and sometimes even chats with Buddy. My co-owner Wendy and her twenty-three-year-old helper came down from Norfolk, Virginia, with several of our puppies. We stayed at a hotel located by "The Villages" located near Ocala, Florida.

One evening my friends and I walked a couple of blocks to the center of the square. This charming area consists of a large paved area which has a large fountain, lovely plantings and an elevated space for the band. I hear the band plays there nightly. This planned elder community is huge with all different housing options. There are lots and lots of activities to fill the time from early morning to late evening. It is like going to a fun upscale adult camp.

I have visited "The Villages" twice and feel I could live there very happily. Hubby says there are too many people and life would be too planned for him. The D.C.A. shows, which used to last four or five days, now go on for eight to nine days. There were two other specialties this year: The Dalmatian Club of Greater Atlanta and The Dalmatian Club of Central Florida. I was a founding member of both clubs, naturally, I just had to support these additional shows. In addition to D.C.A. conformation classes (like the big dog shows you may have seen on television) there are various obedience classes, agility competition plus a road trail competition where the horse's rider owns the dog that runs along with the horse over hill and dale. The Dalmatians and the riders love it. Unfortunately I only saw a small amount of the obedience and agility trials. My main focus has always been the breeding of happy, healthy, beautiful Dalmatians. I took my first show boy to obedience classes to learn "the basics." He did extremely well even though he wasn't as smart as most of the dogs I have had since. The reasons I did not show in obedience (O.B.) are that I always showed on a very limited budget and I did not care for a few of the O.B. people. Years ago some of the people who owned Golden Retrievers seemed, to me to be overly obsessed with making their dogs the perfect performers. It didn't look like fun to me. If I had been younger when they developed the agility classes, I would have probably tried that as it appears to be fun for the dog and owner. I loved conformation especially if my dog beat the dogs, the professional handlers or the big-time very political breeders' dogs. Sometimes politics are just politics. The best dog doesn't always win. Sad but true as new people soon find out. Oh – come on, cookie, you don't think that is fair. Get real – it happens. In the early days when I complained to a friend about this she said, "If it's too hot in the

186

kitchen, get out." But you have to understand that I love breeding and showing too much to give it up. Unfortunately today, I don't run fast enough to keep up with the Dals. Now my co-owner shows the dogs. I do love helping with the planned breedings. With a B.S. degree and over fifty years of experience plus knowledge and memory of old dogs in the pedigrees, I could help our breed.

I really try to help Dal people who are serious about breeding. People who care enough about the future of the breed to study pedigrees and not just breed to dogs that win. Many of the top winners are passing on lots of problems. Unfortunately the top winners are dogs who have owners who can afford lots of expensive advertising and top-notch professional handlers. It breaks my heart to see our beloved breed having more medical problems and personality problems.

Chapter 52 Fun With Restrooms

When a couple of gals head to the restroom we usually have fun conversations. Often about guys, but sometimes hair stylists, clothes, shoes or bags. (Both the kind you carry on your shoulder and old women.) So now any guy reading this know our secrets.

In my many decades of going to restrooms I have pretty much seen it all. Some of them like the Fox Theater in Atlanta have a lot of marble and ornate fixtures. I remember when they had a maid that we tipped as she gave us a towel. However, I haven't been there in twenty years so not sure what is going on now.

Actually Dr. Hottie has a cool bathroom. It has marble with a contemporary bowl, very "with it," clean and modern. Years ago a friend and I went to lunch at a quaint homey restaurant in St. Petersburg, Florida. The restaurant was family owned. Later I found out someone I knew had done the decorating. I could be wrong but I believe it had pink-and-white striped paper above a white chair rail with a rose paper border at the top. They had tropical plants by the doorway with round glass tables and white "ice cream parlor" metal chairs or perhaps white bentwood. The restroom had, I believe, the matching floral paper with a coordinating stripe paper border. As I recall, an old dresser had a marble top with porcelain basins and decorative brass fixtures. It was all well done in a Victorian look. In San Francisco, restaurant restrooms at The Palace Hotel and The St. Frances Hotel were Victorian, done in a deep wine or deep green with fancy Victorian gold mirrors, curved dark granite countertops over even more ornate Victorian-looking cabinetry. As best as I can remember from the late sixties, the St. Frances had ceilings that were very tall and were done in a gold foil with over-the-top crystal chandeliers. The toilets were standard white but the booths were dark mahogany carved like the ones used in the sink area. There was a lady attendant who would hand you a white linen towel to wipe your hands, as she patiently waited for her tip. I also recall there being beautiful live floral arrangements on the long counter between the sinks so the room smelled good.

After we moved to the Atlanta area in April of 1969, and Hubby's mom was in town, we went down to the new modern hotel in the heart of the city. The restroom was super sleek with marble walls, counters, and the front of the cabinet that dropped down was also marble. The hardware was very contemporary with either nickel or brass as were the wall mounted lighting fixtures to accompany ceiling lights that were recessed. Mom and I thought it was very elegant. Makes me wonder if it looks the same now.

These are the lovely restrooms that stand out in my memory. Then there are the horrible ones I had pretty much forgotten about until I decided to write about how I hate porta-potties. I had to use a couple of porta-potties at an Ocala, Florida, horse park. This is where the Dalmatian Club of America held our annual big show in 2016. Even clean, they are less than desirable, aren't they? I think porta-potties are the worst restrooms. I don't hate much but I do hate having to see them and use them. My trusty typist, Leslie, has seen just how very horrible they can be. Leslie and a date went to Jacksonville Beach, Florida, to a blues concert. (It sounded to me like it was a booze/ beer event.) Leslie, like most gals, waited until she couldn't wait anymore. Of course there was a very long line. She said the odor about knocked her over. Some gals and guys didn't hit the mark, shall we say. Pee was everywhere. (You ought to have seen her face when she told me about it.) I was on my way to judge a worldwide dog show when I had the worst restroom experience ever. The experience was twenty years ago at a run- down gas station. I shudder just thinking about it. The restroom was not filthy but it wasn't what I would call clean. But as you know when you have to go – you have to go. I usually sit but no way – this time. After I went I somehow dropped my wallet in my pee. The bowl was rusty and not very clean and I had to reach in there to get it. Ugh, Ugh, big UGH! If you find me a bit crazy, this could be the reason. Then of course I had to wash the wallet, money, cards, etc., then wash and dry my hands. I purchased a new wallet as soon as I could.

P.S. FYI, you need to consider getting an RFD wallet that blocks criminals from scanning your personal information. The scammer equipment is so sophisticated they can walk by your bag hanging on your arm or on a chair and get all your data in a minute without your knowledge.

Chapter 53 *Fun With Bits and Pieces*

Here are a few short stories that were too funny to leave out. Maybe Interesting Stuff!

I read that a guru is someone who has wisdom and gives out advice. If you live as long as I have, you learn "stuff." As a former teacher, isn't it my responsibility to advise people what to do? Maybe, or maybe not. Oh, the book also says a guru is someone of great intelligence – that leaves me out, doesn't it? Hubby noticed something about me that was a surprise. Asking anyone for help is a real pain, isn't it? This is especially true for someone like me who is used to doing almost everything myself. Hubby said that I start out saying, "I need to go to the grocery store." A day later it becomes, "We need to think about going to the grocery store." Finally, Hubby says I will say, "Would you please pick up a few things at the grocery store?" Sometimes I am amused by the things Hubby notices.
Frankly, I wasn't aware I was doing that. Hard to believe, isn't it?

Why is it we hate to ask for help or advice? Strange as it may seem I don't mind asking friends for advice. It is just that I hate to ask for physical help. I hate to admit I can't lift and do everything myself. How about you?

Fun With Our Sons

Years ago my loving mother-in-law advised us to go to church, get involved and find church friends. Years before moving to Florida, she got through some very difficult times with the help of God and church. I believe her really good friends were from church groups. Hubby and I became regular church-goers in Florida and California. When we moved to Georgia we just didn't try hard enough to find the right church. My big regret as a mom is that I didn't push harder to do this. I am grateful our boys turned out to be wonderful men. However, I really feel that as parents, we might have had an easier time with our sons if we had a church family. I think we all would have been happier. Now both of our sons are regular churchgoers and our youngest has worked as a chaplain with Hospice. He hopes to write a book about some of his funny experiences with the dying and their families. I told him the title should be, *Why Are People Dying To Meet Me?* Actually our sons are very caring, very funny and are better writers than I am. Our oldest son gave me his small book, *Ride Across America*, which he wrote about his motorcycle trip from South Georgia to the West Coast. I hope he'll expand it and get it published. He could call his book, *Racing Across the U.S. to Drive My Mom Crazy.* (He did this camping trip by himself which made me very anxious.) He could write about his ten motorcycle/auto accidents! I told you I have wonderful sons. I did not tell you they have been easy, did I?

Our youngest started selling newspapers at ten. At eleven or twelve, after he and I had returned home from a very wet dog show, he got a "brilliant" idea to start a small business. While I was checking out at K-Mart he was waiting for me with a big package. I asked him what he got. He later showed me about ten purple plastic umbrellas. He bought low and planned to make money by selling at other dog shows. Guess what, it never rained at shows again; however, he was always ready if it did. When he left home for the Air Force (seven years) I had

Hubby put all his stuff in the attic. The umbrellas were never seen again till we moved years later. By this time the attic heat had done them in. Hubby and I had a big laugh. I wish I would have wrapped them in gift paper and given them to him for a funny Christmas gift. Our family does things like that. We call these type of gifts "Ho Ho." That way the person knows it is a joke gift.

Fun With Gay Guys

Move over, Kathy Lee Gifford. You're not the only one who loves gay guys! They make wonderful pals, sometimes better than gal pals.

Can you imagine a guy that actually *listens* to you? I've been around a lot of men, Hubby, two sons, one grandson, uncles, cousins and many work acquaintances. Many of them try to listen, if you get my drift. Okay, men in my family act like they are listening but I'm on to them. Bet you twenty-five dollars they couldn't answer questions on what they heard. The eye contact is sort of there but not their minds. They are thinking about football, dinner, how to save the world, or maybe some other things.

I've observed that gay guys usually listen and are a lot more fun. Often at parties, straight guys are checking out the ladies and trying to impress the men. Gay guys who have partners are there to have fun! They may even ask you to dance.

They are also good to take shopping. A lot of them have design backgrounds and will guide you towards clothes that won't make your butt look big. They will tell you the truth about how you look.

If you are planning a party, enlist their help. Either they or some of their gay friends have worked in the restaurant, party or floral business. Be fun, be sweet and they will do just about anything for you.

A couple of years ago Hubby and I went to an Episcopal commitment service (just like a wedding service). There were, I believe, eight or so couples who had been legally married in other states but wanted a real church experience. After the wedding part, a big reception with a dinner dance was held. Girlfriend, I had just about the most fun ever. I've got to mention that I danced with about six guys and a couple of the gay gals, too. Meanwhile, my not-so-fun family sat and watched. Hubby danced with me once. Oh well, he may not be that great a dancer but he really tries to keep me happy. I didn't say he wasn't smart, did I?

Then I have fun with my bookends, Dalmatian guy owners. I usually sit between them because I love good-looking bookends. We always have a good time.

My gay hairdresser is always amusing. He told me about a Halloween party he had gone to a few years ago. A guy friend came as Britney Spears with a baby doll strapped to his leg and pantyhose made to look like afterbirth dragging along after him. I would have loved to see that, wouldn't you?

One of my best work buddies I met in the decorating business. Since our sense of humor is similar, we often crack each other up. We can almost finish the other's sentence. The relationship has been going on over forty years. We love telling one another true crazy-people stories.

Even though I write for gal pals, I hear the gay guys like my books too! Having a great gay guy friend is like having a great old dog you love dearly. They listen to you and want to do about anything you want to do. P.S. I haven't found one who chases balls yet. Have you?

Fun With Ghosts

A reader of my "Panties" book recently told me that when she lost her father she had the most interesting experience. After her father died she couldn't sleep and ended up lying on the sofa crying. All of a sudden she stopped and opened her eyes. Before her on a blank wall were new baseball-sized colored dots. She said, "Dad, is that you?" The colored dots started dancing around. It was then that she knew her dad was okay.   A few months later my friend had an upsetting call from her mother. Her mom was in tears as she had received a three thousand-dollar tax bill. She had no idea how she would pay it. My friend told her mom they would figure it out when she got back into town.

Soon my friend and her husband were on the road. She asked her husband if they could stop by to visit her dad's grave. Then she asked her husband to help her decide what she could do to help her mom. She didn't want to spend more than her set-aside vacation money. She played the slots and was ready to quit when she found a twenty-dollar bill she didn't know she had. The very next play she hit the "jackpot' and made more than her mom needed to pay the taxes. A bit weird, but she swore it was all true.

Have you read my personal ghost stories in my *Hold on to Your Panties and Have Fun* book? You might find it really interesting.

Fun With Unusual Sights

Sometimes I accidentally hear weird stories. How about the story of the old man who was visiting a North Carolina Shoney's on a Sunday morning with his family. He apparently went to the restroom only to come out NUDE and proceeded to stroll around the breakfast bar in his birthday suit. Apparently he was dealing with dementia.

Last week I heard about a NUDE guy who drove up to a local Florida drive-through liquor window. The owner was clearly able to see a full view of his "jewels." The nude guy knew the clerk was able to see everything.

He paid for his beer with money and a smile.

Speaking of nude, a relative told me it is not wise to have sex on the beach as the sand gets in places you definitely do not want grit.

P.S. Southern gals say "nekked" for naked, instead of nude.

Somehow naked sounds more risqué, doesn't it?

Chapter 54 *Fun With Elizabeth The Great and The Royals*

The Queen of England, after the Diamond Jubilee, is now known to her subjects as Elizabeth the Great. I remember when she took the throne. I, more than ten years younger, remember her face gracing the cover of Life Magazine. This was a large, popular magazine, maybe eighteen-by-twenty inches in size.

Many thought the Queen was a very attractive young lady. I thought her a real beauty when I saw her from twelve to fifteen feet away in 1974. She was forty-eight years old. The Queen and Prince Philip were in a limo as they came through the palace gates. She wore a robin's egg blue coat and matching pillbox hat, like Jackie O's. Being short-wasted with large boobies, she appeared bigger in photos than in real life. She always looked somewhat frumpy and much heavier. She probably wore a size four. She had lovely porcelain skin. Her clothes at the time were tasteful and of course beautifully made; however, photos showed her wearing knee-length dresses when most of us were wearing ours a bit shorter. Now she looks like she has been in a "time warp." She still has a lovely figure and apparently has good health. Wonder what she would look like with a little hair color, better makeup and Kate's stylist? WOW!

Did any of you see the Diamond Jubilee Celebrations? Wasn't it fabulous? I noticed the music was very contemporary. I also observed that the Palace had a facelift. I told a friend, "Too bad the Queen didn't have one too." Ha ha. Okay, you English people, don't get your panties in a wad. It's a JOKE!

Wondering why Queenie is still carrying a handbag all the time. Question, since her clothes are custom-made, couldn't she have inside pockets for her lipstick, etc.? It's not like she needs to carry several Kotex. Okay, I get it. Maybe she needs an extra pair of Depends. Bless her heart!
But does she need ID?

So you think I am being too hard on the Queen? Just think of how good Betty White looks. She is older than the Queen. The Queen is the wealthiest woman in the world. You know she has more money than Betty and maybe more money than God. If you had that much money wouldn't you do everything to stay as good-looking as possible?

Say, girlfriend, it takes a lot less energy and time to go natural, but sweetheart, we have to look at you! If I can get my hair colored and put on make-up every day at my age, can't you?

Did you know that the Queen of England has bred several different types of horses? Race horses, polo ponies and performance horses? One of her most important horses was a performance horse. It was the horse the Queen's daughter, Princess Anne, rode in the Olympics. From time to time, the press will mention a big horse race often is won by a horse belonging to the Queen. The English love their pets. This dates back to Queen Victoria who adored her animals. The Royal Society for Prevention of Cruelty to Animals was actually founded before the English Child Protection League. It is kind of interesting that the English appeared to care more for their pets than their children. Hey, I've been around thousands of dogs and a number of cats, and I have to tell you animals are usually a lot more fun than most kids, and possibly the Queen. Sidebar: Am I the only one who sees parents who don't know how to make their children behave? Aren't there books and videos that could help them? Did you know you can teach a dog not to bark and a kid not to have a temper tantrum with a spray of water? It works better with a lower, stern voice saying, "No bark," or to a child, "We don't do that."

Royals love their birds. Did you know there are royal swans, now protected, but at one time they were "dinner?" The English had a pair of racing pigeons to accompany every fighter plane in World War II. The purpose was to send a message back to England, if the plane was shot down. The pigeons could be sent back with the plane's location. These pigeons were credited with saving many lives. Who knew the Queen currently owns two to three hundred pigeons? They are regularly raced and win prizes. Who knew pigeons could be so well trained?

The royals adore their dogs. The Queen is often seen with her Corgis; Princess Anne, with her Dachshunds. There was even a scandal, as one of Princess Anne's Dachshunds had an "accidental" breeding with one of the queen's Corgis. The one I saw on television looked like a long-haired Dachshund. The head was a bit wider with upright ears of the Corgi. I saw a photo of the Queen and Prince Philip with this offspring. Interesting that the royals did not keep the bitch confined during her season. That wasn't responsible. It NEVER IS!

We don't need more dogs filling up the shelters, do we?

P.S. Queenie, maybe you need to check those bitches or teach your daughter how to keep hers up, or spay and neuter if you aren't responsible. P.P.S. I do love you, Queenie, but you're not my type, sorry.

Chapter 55 *Fun With Scents and Flowers*

You want to feel happier, go for a walk, preferably among the trees. If it's snowing or you live at the beach, you may want to go for scented plants such as a wax plant and eucalyptus. To lower your blood pressure and heart rate, try scented spring flowers.

It works somehow by releasing and relaxing certain neurotransmitters, according to Dr. Alan Hirsch. Apparently there was a hospital test that showed positive results in their patients. According to the article I read, breathing the aroma of spring flowers will relax you and helps with sleep.

Rose, lavender, lilac and jasmine are said to have the most tension reduction. Yard work is especially good for us as it's not only relaxing, it gets you out in the sun, works some muscles and makes you happy to see the fruits of your labor. Looking and working in a pretty yard with colorful blooms is a mood lifter.

Did you know that a just-mowed yard allows the blade of grass to emit some mood-lifting molecules? Our brain's memory and emotions center is enhanced and energized by the negative ions. With every breath we take in more revitalizing oxygen. It is the same as a spring or summer shower. These ions, also produced from a hot shower, can reduce chronic fatigue up to sixty percent. Allergy and respiratory problems are also reduced by these ions. In my readings I came across an article about how women are like various flowers. For instance, the chrysanthemum type gal is sturdy, capable and usually a very good friend. She often has a long-term gal life partner. I've been a little jealous of these chrysanthemums' capabilities. Frankly, one I knew could knock down walls, remodel and make furniture. The chrysanthemum is often very capable professionally too. One I knew was a doctor. This type of gal is usually devoted to her partner and is a good friend, if you don't interfere with her significant other. Beware not to get friendlier with one than the other.

The day lily is the type who is emotionally very fragile. She is probably beautiful, spending a lot of time and effort on "her looks." She will have repeated facelifts and perhaps liposuction to remove unwanted fat. She will sacrifice a lot to keep herself looking young. The day lilies I've known are wholesome and sweet. They normally are great friends but maybe not you're most intellectual friend, and they can be needy.

Black-eyed Susan's will scrap with you about anything. They are ALWAYS right. (Like my mother.) You may be friends with her, but keep your guard up and try not to argue. You have to say, "You have a point," then change the subject. If you have similar views on most things you'll get along fine. If not, be prepared like a Boy Scout!

The magnolia is kind, like the Quakers I knew growing up. They are down to earth and don't require much in life. They are usually happy with less than others. They make wonderful friends. They are hard workers and work hard at all their relationships. They are kind of "the salt of the earth" types – honest and good to the core. They are the opposite of the "good consumer" types. My paternal grandmother was one. She never complained about her life. She was very active in church, but without the "holier than thou" attitude. She was loyal to her family, friends and a pillar of the community. Maybe she could have been a better mother-in-law??? My parents, with three children, had moved into the family home. Grandmother came down the lane from the small, formerly tenant house twice every day to milk her cows and check on her chickens. She would frequently stop in at the house – possibly to hang out with her oldest granddaughter, me, or my brother and little sister. One day my mother happened, so she said, to find my grandmother snooping through my parents' dresser drawers. Mother wasn't amused. I'm not sure if they had words or my mother kept quiet. (I never heard them argue.)

The only time I saw or heard of Grandmother being upset was after her husband ran over one of her chickens. Grandfather was well over six feet, a red-headed Scot. He didn't seem like an easy man to live with; however, he was kind to everyone – just not pleasant. There is a difference; I do know you didn't want to cross him. He could yell loudly, and I believe he had a short fuse. Grandmother told us, "I'll show him. He killed my chicken, so I'm going to buy new living room curtains." That was the end of their feud, I believe. I never heard them argue but this was probably due to my grandmother's genuine sweetness. Too bad I am not more like her.

The daisy is kind of like a lot of the girls we saw in the forties and fifties movies, the girl next door, like June Allyson. That is sweet, cute, a good friend, down to earth, good-natured and easygoing. There's not a lot around like June anymore. The Queen Anne's lace type of gal is one that some men dream of. The kind that wear lace or ruffled underwear and fuss over a man, almost suffocating him. She makes a good friend if she has time for you after doing everything for and with her man. She clings to him like she is nothing without him. She always has to check "their schedule" before allowing herself any time away from him. She could, despite her very feminine appearance, be gay. In any event don't get between her and hers, if you get my drift.

The tiger lily is usually a sultry kind of sexy, well-dressed gal even if she has few clothes. She makes the most of what she has. Even if overweight, she turns heads. Both males and females are captured by her "certain something." I've known and witnessed this with two older, ample gals. Both were extremely charming; however, in both cases when they walked into a room of strangers, most people would turn to look at them. Neither were beauties; however, both had big boobs and loads of charisma. They were about five feet, five inches, to five feet, seven inches, tall, but had good posture and wore their clothes well; neither were over-dressed or in expensive clothes. It was amazing to be with them. Man-oh-man, were they man-magnets.

One was a close friend for years until she died. The other I hung out with on a cruise. In spite of being dealt several difficult hands in life, Sarah was one of my best friends. Both gals oozed confidence. I'm a taller, not ugly, well-dressed older gal with confidence that has never had heads turn.
I really don't get it, do you? Ha, ha.

The daffodil flower is one of the first to raise its head in spring. Like the flower, the daffodil person tries to be stunning in appearance. This requires much shopping and usually a high credit card balance. Maybe she returns clothes after she decides what her best looks are for the season. She may change friends often, especially if her husband changes jobs or is transferred a lot. Possibly this is because as she stuffs her closet, she kind of suffocates herself with too many friends. She loves her girlfriends, is charming and loves girlfriend shopping trips. However, she is never happy with how she looks. "I'm so heavy I can't stand it." She buys, and buys and buys, her closets stuffed but NEVER has anything to wear. She is the gal who often obsesses about bags and shoes.

Why does she do this??? I don't know why anyone wants to put themselves into big debt unless maybe they are trying to fill a void of some kind.

Question: Is stuffing closets – hoarding???   P.S. Did Jesus ever change his clothes or did he wear them dirty? I'm just asking, okay?

P.P.S. When I read these chapters to my friend, she said, "I guess I'm the whole bouquet." (We are all parts of more than one flower, don't you think?)

Chapter 56 Fun With My O.B.

Who, I ask you, can write your obituary better than you? To save some of your family the stress of doing it and to include all the information that might be of interest, why not write it yourself? This could be the basis for my O.B. and of course I just need to croak for it to be used. (I wrote mine like I am gone.)

Emily Joanne Cleland Hoover was born February 24, 1935, outside a small southern town in Ohio. Her parents were Lee and Rose Cleland. Emily was born at her grandparents' home and delivered by a female physician. A female doctor was very unusual in 1935. Twenty months later her brother, Larry, was born. Her sister, Gloria, arrived when Emily was in the first grade. Emily was named after her aunt but was called Joanne until she went off to college. She grew up in the country in southern Ohio. Her father was a soil conservation consultant for the U.S. government. Her mother, a homemaker.

In 1953 she entered Mary Washington College in Fredericksburg, Virginia. A year later she transferred to The OSU. She received a Bachelor of Science degree in education in 1957. After college she was hired as a lighting consultant for Dayton Power and Light Company in Dayton, Ohio. On July 6, 1958, she married her college sweetheart. He was an engineer for United Air Craft in Hartford, Connecticut, where they lived for about eight months.

In February of 1959 they moved to St. Petersburg, Florida, and in June became parents to their first son. Emily was soon teaching evening adult classes in interior design. A year later she taught at Oak Grove Junior High. Side note: This school was the first one in Florida to have built-in air conditioning. It was part of a study to find out if air conditioning helped students to focus, etc.

In 1961 the Hoovers purchased a new home in Clearwater, Florida. In 1962 the Hoovers welcomed their second son. At that time Emily taught junior high one year, then went back to teaching evening classes for adults, to have more time for their sons. She also was vice president of a large Clearwater branch of the American Association of University Women. During this time Emily decorated several model homes featured in the Better Homes Parade of Homes.

In the fall of 1965 the Hoovers moved to Santa Clara, California, and bought a townhouse. Emily's husband, while at

Walkins-Johnson, earned a few more patents. Emily taught at San Jose High School. After two years they bought a house, maybe Emily's all-time favorite, in Los Altos, California.

In early 1969 a Ph.D. Hubby had worked with in Florida offered him a position with his new startup company, Electro Magnetic Science, Inc.

(EMS) in Atlanta, Georgia.

During this time the Hoovers purchased their first show Dalmatian, "Love." She became their first champion and the foundation for Atlantis Dalmatians. Emily and her Hubby had many Dal meetings and parties that were instrumental in founding The Dalmatian Club of Greater Atlanta.

The Hoovers bought a house in Tucker, Georgia, later selling it and moving to Roswell, Georgia, where they had eight acres and more room for their boys and dogs.

Due to severe allergies (shots for forty-two years), she would escape to the Clearwater, Florida, area to a small place north of Clearwater. Unfortunately, after having the flu, she developed kidney failure and was hospitalized for three weeks; this was very expensive. They had to sell their little cottage. Back in Roswell Emily taught design and fashion classes for The Atlanta School of Art and Design and also did some market research. Unfortunately, she had several surgeries, among them, grade I ovarian cancer, a broken arm, gall bladder and an appendectomy. She was in a bad auto accident resulting in broken ribs and vertebrae. She faced long recoveries. Her attitude had always been, "Pick yourself up and keep going on with your life."

During the eighties both the Hoovers' sons married. In 1983 the Hoovers welcomed their only grandson. In 1989 the Hoovers built a retirement home near Jacksonville, Florida. Since Hubby was not ready to retire they also bought a townhouse in Norcross, Georgia, near his work. Meanwhile they went back and forth between their homes. After a visit to Franklin, North Carolina they decided to sell the townhouse in Norcross, and buy a small house there, since Hubby was semi-retired. During the summers Mr. Hoover would leave North Carolina on Mondays and arrive at his desk in Norcross, Georgia, about 10:00 A.M. to return on Friday afternoon. During the winter he did most his work on a computer from Florida. (Amazing at eighty he was still getting some part-time work resulting in more patents.)

During this time Emily was busy writing books. Her first, *Hold On To Your Panties And Have Fun,* was self-published at the end of 2011. Her next book was *I Hate Porta-Potties, Sprinkles And Tight Underwear.* Her books were primarily about fun life adventures that she witnessed or caused to happen. Her decorating book, *Decorating Isn't A Joke, Or Is It?,* was started as a textbook with a college professor friend.

This was about the time the Hoovers moved to California. Both women were very busy in an age before e-mail was available. Long-distance calls were super-expensive so the book was put on hold. Emily decided to make the decorating book a fun do-it-yourself book.

Emily had always loved music marching bands, especially brass, jazz, jive and jitterbug. But most of all she enjoyed meeting all the people God sent into her life. When young she was active in 4-H club and was the outstanding 4-H girl in Fayette County, Ohio, at the age of sixteen. In grade school, high school and college Emily played the cornet. She played in a dance band while in Mary Washington College. Emily was an active member of the Junior Women's Club in Clearwater, Santa Clara and Los Alto, California. She was on the board of the Los Altos Methodist church. She took extension courses from the University of Florida, San Jose State, the University of Northern California, San Francisco State and the University of Georgia. Emily was also active in the American Association of University Women (A.A.U.W.) serving as vice president of the Clearwater branch and later president in Roswell.

Emily was known as a gal who loved teasing people who came into her life – especially guys. She loved having fun with her friends, painting in acrylics/oils, doing book signings, decorating, breeding and showing her Atlantis Dalmatians, home projects, jitterbugging, designing furniture, clothing, judging dogs, reading and meeting new people. However, she most of all loved spending time with family and friends. If this involved wine or margaritas, so much the better.

Emily was a founding member of both the Dalmatian Club of Greater Atlanta and the Mid-Florida Dalmatian Club. She was also a long-time member of the Dalmatian Club of America and co-breeder of an all-breed Best in Show winner. Two more Best in Show Winners have her breeding in their lineage.

Emily has been a member of the Art Association in Roswell, Georgia, and an art organization in Florida. She was also a member of the Florida Writers Association and Writers by the Sea, as well as a local Newcomers Club. She leaves her family, many friends and her devoted Dalmatian – Diva.

Chapter 57 *Fun In Rural Ohio*

When I was nine we moved to our paternal grandparents' family farm, which had been in the family for several generations. There were a couple of barns and a fourteen room Craftsman house with pillars and a wraparound porch with gray slate siding. We kids loved having lots of room to run around to play or escape to read a book. I really value my alone time now, probably due to living in that house. It had three exterior doors, one to the kitchen, one to the living room on one side and an additional one on the north side of the living room. Inside the living room there was a doorway to the kitchen, one to the dining room as well as a door to the music room. It also faced north and was quite unusual in shape, wider at one end than the other. It had an upright piano and room for us kids to play. Going from the living room into the dining room you were aware that the dining room had six doors. It had a door to the large coat or "cloak" (as my grandmother called it) room. Next to the kitchen door was a door to the downstairs bathroom, which had a toilet and sink. Nearby was a bedroom containing a double bed, night-stand and dresser. There may have been a very small closet. I think this was Grandma and Grandpa's bedroom in their later years before they moved from the big house, up the lane to the re-done tenant house.

Upstairs on the left was a bedroom my parents occupied. At the head of the stairs, an old Victorian bathroom complete with claw foot tub, (no shower) and standing sink. The walls were white; I believe the floor had black and white hexagon tile. On the other side were three bedrooms; the largest, my sister and I shared. Our parents purchased new maple twin beds, night-stands and a shared dresser. Mother and Daddy painted our room pale blue. We had white chenille bedspreads and white sheer curtains, and I believe blue throw rugs. On the ceiling Mother put star decals that absorbed light during the day, gradually fading at night. (It was calming to watch the stars as we fell asleep.) Another bedroom, set aside for guests, was across from our bedroom.   In between these rooms was a door that led to the "seed corn" room. It was kind of like an attic – old rough wood floor with several windows facing the north. It contained a couple of large wooden bins that held the corn for the spring plantings. I remember playing "school" in this room. It had a narrow door with steps going up to the attic, which was dark and dusty and a place to store Christmas tree ornaments.

Our very, very small country town was about one mile away with a very small general store, a school with one to twelve grades, and several churches, and some old houses. This was a place where everyone knew who we were and we understood we were from "good people." This home was where I grew up from age nine to fourteen, until my grandfather died. This was the house my dad and his brothers grew up in, the house my grandparents and great-grandparents had lived in. Grandma decided she wanted her younger son to live in this house so we needed to move. My parents found a small farm to buy about thirty-five miles away. It broke my heart to leave our old place. Today thirty-five miles seems like a short distance but I rarely saw any of my friends again.

Sidebar: My third-grade friend Joy and I still keep in touch via birthday calls and Christmas notes. We used to celebrate our birthdays together – hers February twenty-second and mine on the twenty-fourth.

To move to a community where NO ONE knew us was very difficult for me. What really upset me was in our old community, the seventh and eighth grades changed classes with the high school kids. I was in band with most of my older friends. The school I moved to was a two-room school, first through fourth in one room and fifth through eighth in another. I thought I was beyond that. I was the only eighth grade girl with four classmates – all boys. I was active in 4-H activities, band, church, etc. I was in the in-group where I hung out with juniors and seniors in our old community. After moving I was in a room all day with little kids and my very smart brother. He and I continued to be at the top of our classes. My brother and sister and I continued our 4-H and farm bureau activities winning our share of awards. I'm sure he was smarter than I. When living in Martinsville I felt the family and community love.

Unfortunately the family farm was passed on to my uncle; thus Dad got no inheritance except for good genetics and an education. The farm was eventually sold. My sister arranged for our family to go see our old home. It had been remodeled and was in great condition but much smaller than I had remembered.

I felt blessed to see it again and to remember the fun times we had there.

Chapter 58 Fun With Buster

Buster was a fun, very lightly marked Dalmatian, who I got back three times. (Good breeders always take their dogs back if it doesn't work out.) The first owner adored their puppy but when he was about nine months old, a divorce caused mom and her two sons to move to a smaller house without a fenced yard. She had to go back to work. I understood. I soon found his next home with a junior who was about fifteen. Her mom raised Shih Tzu's. Daughter was to be responsible for Buster; however, she became more interested in boys. Buster was loved but wasn't mom's dog and he was a handful so back he came. Soon I sold him to a single thirties guy who while working kept him in his pool enclosure. He adored Buster, but when he went through the screening for the second time he came back to me with ringworm. I kept him separated from my other dogs and treated him, being very careful not to get ringworm myself. Of course I couldn't sell him until he was well. Whenever I let him out I had to make sure my other dogs were crated so they wouldn't get ringworm too. One day I let him out and when I whistled for him to come in I heard what sounded like a herd of buffalos. Wagging their tails, in came Top Spot and Buster all happy to see me. I had forgotten I had let Tops out the back door. He had never been introduced to Buster; however, they both came wagging their tails like best buddies.

Fortunately Tops didn't get ringworm.

Soon I took Buster, Top Spot, his sister Flash and her young daughter, My My, back with me to Georgia. Normally I let one of the girls out with one of the boys. All was well until

Hubby said he wanted me to sell either Tops or Buster. Soon I decided to take Buster with me to California to the Dalmatian Club of America shows.

We arrived at the Atlanta airport bright and early with all the business people flying off to away places. Buster seemed to think all these people were there to see him off. The airlines put Buster in his crate and, surprising to me, put it on the merry-go-round with the California-bound luggage. He acted like it was so much fun, not afraid as some dogs might have been.

He and I arrived, I believe, at the Hilton across the street from Disneyland. Buster seemed very interested in where he was and all that was going on. He seemed fascinated by the very large mats on either side of the main front entrance. He looked from left to right as the doors would open.

A day or so later while my friends were visiting with another friend on the balcony, I took a short shower while the dogs played in the room, when I came out about ten to fifteen minutes later – NO BUSTER. I asked the girls where he was. Fearing the worst, one of them said, "I thought he was in the bathroom with you." "NO." Maybe the maid let him out. I was SUPER upset! One of them said she would check out this floor. I went to look over the balcony thinking he may have jumped over the railing for some reason. I could imagine him lying there dead. I was a basket case. No sign of Buster! One sister said she would go down to the lobby to see if anyone saw him. She claims that before she could push the elevator down button, the doors opened and out comes a happy tail wagging Buster. She got hold of his collar as he happily came back into the room.

The next part of the Buster story took almost five years to piece together. We never figured out how he got downstairs from the fourth floor. However the girls later admitted their bitch could turn doorknobs. Buster was "spotted" lifting his leg in the potty/exercise area. Someone almost caught him when he crossed the hotel driveway to kiss the "little girls" in the ring. The judge was Esmee Treen and she was not amused. Someone grabbed him that had previously come up to the room to look at him. The guy recognized Buster, and took him to the front desk to call my room. About this time the elevator doors opened and Buster escaped him and ran into the elevator. The guy waited for the elevator to come down but Buster wasn't on it. That was probably when one of my roommates grabbed him.

I sold Buster a few days later to a teenage girl and her single mom. The girl showed him some and although he had points toward his championship he never finished. I guess school activities got in the way. I knew that their primary reason for getting him was as a pet. Buster deserved this forever home with people who appreciated an attractive fun pet.

Twenty-plus years later people still laugh about fun and funny Buster.

Chapter 59 *Fun Speeding Down the Four-Lane*

In the fall of 2010, I was driving from North Carolina to south of Atlanta to a dog show. Of course I was late and driving fast – probably ten miles over the speed limit. When a white truck raced past me, I sped up. The truck driver soon put on his brakes and slowed down. So did I. Maybe not fast enough. The cop came across the median and came up on me with lights flashing. The white truck was gone. I pulled over and quickly removed my (apparently not working) radar detector. As I did I was praying, with both my index fingers and thumbs, touching, forming circles around the steering wheel. (That is supposed to connect you with God.) The "handsome" young cop was suddenly on my right leaning against my van. He said, "How are you?" I wanted to say, "How in the hell do you think I am?" - But of course I didn't. I said, "I'm fine." He then said, "I stopped you for going over the speed limit." I replied, with my most innocent look, "Oh." He then said, "I need to see your driver's license." I handed it to him. "Wow, we just came back from there on our vacation. The beach sure is nice." I said, "We were blessed to buy there before it got too expensive." He said, "I need your registration, please." I opened my glove compartment and began going through everything. I said, "I have all these receipts from the work I have had done on my van. It is thirteen years old and I try to keep it in top condition." I kept searching and going through papers.

I came across a real cool photo I was given – probably twenty-five years ago in Roswell, Georgia, at Fox Photo. This photo was taken by the woman who gave it to me. She told me it was taken after a hurricane had gone up the coast of South Carolina. It shows a sailboat tipped over. What makes it unusual is that when you turn the photo sideways, on the other side you can see an image that looks like Christ. I handed it to "the" cop as I told him the story. He thought it remarkable too. I said, "I'm in trouble here as I can't find my registration." He handed me the photo and said, "That is a remarkable photo. I'll take your license and see if I can pull it up. Florida is tricky to pull up." I was praying away. He came back and handed me my license and said, "Just back it down and stay within the speed limit." I said, "Yes, sir. Thank you." I rolled my window up then said, "Thank you, God! Thank you, God!" I didn't speed for at least ten minutes – okay, maybe eight.   P.S. Don't do as I do – do as you should, okay?

Chapter 60 *Fun at the Love's Truck Stop*

Apparently there is a lot of soliciting going on at the Love's Truck Stop – or at least that is what I hear about one in South Georgia. Sidebar: I do have friends that tell me stuff they hear, supposedly from good sources. It is not what you know but what you hear – sometimes.

Some time ago I met a gal at a local outdoor restaurant/bar. I like to sit at the bar and look out at the water. Hubby had gone to North Carolina so I was on my own. I especially like this restaurant's sweet potato fries. They slice the potatoes like you would for potato chips, not like the ones cut lengthwise and skinny. I also love their burgers. I get mine without a bun. I usually order coleslaw, which my readers know is my favorite salad. Sidebar: Hubby and I frequent this restaurant for lunch so we know a lot of the servers/bartenders. It is a family-friendly place. Thus I don't feel strange going to the bar about five o'clock or so for a wine and dinner when he is out of town. A gal I didn't know joined me and soon we were chatting. By now you know I like to talk to strangers, even some a bit strange. I'll tell you this. I have met the most interesting people because of my outgoing mouth.

This gal told me she met a very interesting truck driver on the internet. After a few months they would occasionally call each other. He lived in Tampa, she in north Florida. Nothing came of their relationship until about two years later when her new job took her to the west coast, St. Petersburg west of Tampa. She called him up and he said it was time they met – Guess where? At a Love's Truck Stop south of Tampa. They met up and sparks flew. He had a delivery and he asked her to go with him. They talked and talked on the road and later at a restaurant bar near the Love's Truck Stop where she had left her car.

This happened to be New Year's Eve. After hours of chatting and dancing they returned to her car. Did she drive back to St. Pete? No, they did the rock-n-roll in his truck right there at the Love's Truck Stop! Soon he moved to north Florida and in with "Ms. Fun." As far as I know they are still together a couple of years later.

P.S. I hear the Love's Truck Stop has some of the best gas prices. I'm just saying – anything can happen at that place.   P.P.S. Don't I meet the most interesting people?

Chapter 61 *Fun With Fast Cars, Vans and Tricycles*

By now you probably know I like the fast lane and fast vehicles. (Fast-talking guys not so much.) At the moment I lust, yes, God, lust after the Porsche Boxster. Most gals aren't as interested in sports cars as I am. I love sports cars and talking cars to guys.

There has been an older silver Boxster for sale in our local paper. Although ten-plus years, it looks like it has been well taken care of and has less than thirty thousand miles. They want about twenty-four thousand dollars – roughly half of the original price. No, I haven't seen it. Will I? No, I don't want car payments and I need my van for carrying lovely Diva, the Dalmatian, and all my stuff when I travel. I did meet a gal who had a bright yellow Boxster. She and her fabulous car were outside my vet's office when I was picking up my dog's heartworm and flea meds. The Boxster was so cool and so was the owner. We had a short lively chat, but had we met at a bar or restaurant we could have had lots of fun.   According to my youngest son, the Boxster is very popular with either very successful forty- to sixty-year-old women or older gals as part of their divorce settlement. I believe my son to be a real car guy. He was sixteen when I helped him buy his first car, a used 1971 red Datsun (made in Japan.) Since then he and his family have owned:

1971 Datsun 1200 (Japan)

1981 Dodge Colt (Japan)

1967 Opel Rekor (Germany)

1983 Daihatsu Charade (Japan)

1985 Volvo 240 (Sweden)

1984 Toyota Corolla (Japan)

1985 Subaru Turbo (Japan)

1986 Toyota Tercel (Japan)

1988 Chevy Corsica (USA)

1991 Mercury Capri (Australia)

1991 Oldsmobile Custom Cruiser (USA)

1993 Mercury Capri (Australia)

1996 VW Passat (Germany)

1997 Ford Expedition (USA)

1997 Ford Aspire (Korea)

2000 Jeep Grand Cherokee (USA)

2001 Chevrolet Prizm (USA)

2000 Chrysler Sebring (USA)

1997 Buick Riviera (USA)

1998 Jeep Grand Cherokee (USA)

2002 Buick Rendezvous (Mexico)

2004 Buick Rendezvous (Mexico)

2006 Cadillac SRX (USA)

2008 Buick Enclave (USA)

2012 Chevy Volt (USA)

2014 Buick Encore (Korea)

2017 Chevy Traverse (USA)

2017 Chevy Cruz (Mexico)

2018 Buick Regal TourX (Germany)

At one time he took not one, not two, but four car magazines. (I used to enjoy reading interesting car articles while visiting him.)

Speaking of sports cars, Hubby and I saw a brand new Panoz at a 2015 car show. The one we saw was the "Panoz Esperante Spyder." It was the Twenty-fifth Anniversary Edition. It was red and ready to roll to the tune of two hundred thousand dollars. Have you ever seen one? I had not, yet the company has been making them for twenty-five years. They are low, sleek and just damn beautiful, baby! The 2015 Panoz "Spyder" can be complete custom-made to order just for you. You have engine choices from four hundred thirty to eight hundred horsepower. Each car is one of a kind. They have beautiful interior dash woods, supple leathers and can be painted whatever color you want. Brushed aluminum as well as high-tech carbon fiber in this American original.

The Spyder is said to be the fastest, lightest sports car ever produced. It is definitely a highly desirable "dream car." It is made in America, actually north of Atlanta in Hoschton, Georgia. Should you have LOTS of money to purchase, look them up at www.panoz.com. Remember they start at two hundred thousand dollars but you can get one to match your nail polish or your red hair. That's custom! The smart looking California salesperson told me that most of them are sold in California, thirty-five last year. Now let's see, if they make one hundred thousand dollars profit, that's not bad. Too bad I'm not younger – I could sell you one maybe the color of money. Ha ha.

Another car guy I was talking to told me that people who have very expensive cars drive around in them but never park. They don't want them to get stolen, keyed or dinged. Those are worries you and I don't have, right?

I've thought of having the top cut out of my van and adding a canvas top to make it into a van-convertible. It's red. I love sitting up higher. With long legs, low sitting seats in sports cars aren't so comfortable and they are difficult to get in and out of. Maybe I could start a new trend with my van convertible. What do you think? Hubby thinks I'm crazy. Now what about a really fast motorized tricycle? The manufacturers call them motorcycles but I see more and more old people on the three- and four-wheeled ones. These old guys haven't gotten better looking with age. Most were rather short to begin with; now you can add stocky and often ugly gray hair to their descriptions. What can I say, I like to look at younger guys – legal eye candy.

You are talking ugly, Emily. Well, I tell it like it is, don't I? You were secretly thinking the same thing yourself, right?

I have a friend who has an eighty-five-year-old husband who drives her crazy. He drives his motorcycle from west of Asheville, North Carolina, to outside of Washington, D.C., to meet up with his nephew for a road trip. He does not go on the interstate highways, nor does he drive after dark. Nevertheless, it is scary to think about, isn't it? I'm just glad he isn't my husband. Some would say crazy fun old guy who doesn't hear well, but my friend has loved him for over sixty years. Why? I'm not sure as he has always been a bit self-serving.

Chapter 62 *Fun With Recipes*

Zesty Sweet/Sour Sauce

2/3 Cup Firmly Packed Brown Sugar	2 Tbl. Flour
2/3 Cup Pineapple Juice	1 Tsp. Water
1 ½ Tsp. Brown Mustard	1 Tsp. Soy Sauce

1 Cup Vinegar

Combine sugar and flour in pan over medium heat. Slowly add pineapple juice. After moistening with water, stir into pan along with vinegar and soy sauce. Bring to a boil. (Can be enjoyed with sausage balls or shrimp.

Leslies' Holiday Pumpkin Spread

¾ Cup Cream Cheese (room temp)   2 Tbl. Maple Syrup

½ Cup Packed Brown Sugar   ½ Tsp. Cinnamon

½ Cup Canned Pumpkin

Mix all ingredients until smooth. Chill thirty minutes. Can be served with apple slices or pretzels for a mouth-watering holiday snack.

Joni's Perfect Margarita

2 oz. Silver Tequila   ¼ oz. Grand Marnier

¼ oz. Cointreau   ¼ oz. Triple Sec

½ oz. Orange Juice 1 oz. Sweet & Sour or Margarita Mix

Blend with shaved ice in a blender until desired consistency. Serve in salt rimmed glasses.

Fun Pineapple Rum

1 ½ oz. Pineapple Flavored Rum

½ oz. Pineapple Juice

1 oz. Cream of Coconut

½ oz. Coconut

Water

½ Lime Juice

Blend with ice and serve.

Leslie's Orange Balsamic Salad

Spring Lettuce Mixture   Blond Raisins

Apple Chunks, Peeled and Cored Orange Balsamic Vinegar

Orange Slices, Save the Juice Olive Oil

Small Nuts or Chopped Walnuts Red Onions Sliced into Rings

Toss lettuce, apples, oranges, raisins and onions, tip with nut mixture. Drizzle with olive oil and vinegar.

Terry's Green Pea Salad

½ Cup Thawed Frozen Peas   ½ Cup Bacon Bits
Shredded Lettuce   1/8 Cup Chopped Onion
¼ Cup Chopped Celery   2 Tsp. Sugar
1 Cup Mayonnaise   Parmesan Cheese

Mix first seven ingredients then top with Parmesan cheese. Refrigerate for at least one hour.

Julie's Easy Crock Pot BBQ Pork

2 Lb. Pork Roast or   Southern Style Dry Rub
4 Boneless Chicken Breasts BBQ Sauce of Choice

Southern Style Dry Rub

1 Tsp. Cayenne Pepper
¼ Cup Dark Brown Sugar ¼ Cup Paprika
¼ Cup Coarse Salt   2 Tbl. Black Pepper
2 Tsp. Garlic Powder   2 Tbl. Onion Powder
Whisk ingredients together then store in airtight container.

Coat then massage the dry rub on meat, then place in zip lock storage bag. Refrigerate overnight. Place meat into crock pot with one cup of water. Cook on high setting for five to six hours, then on low for seven to eight hours. When meat is done, shred using forks, then coat with BBQ Sauce.

Ann's Easy Beef Roast

1 Beef Roast, Any Cut   1 2/3 Cup Water
1 Can Cream of Mushroom Soup
½ Packet Onion Soup Mix

Mix soup, water and onion soup mix powder together to make a paste. Place roast in roasting pan and cover with soup mixture. Roast until preferred doneness. Extra gravy is delicious served on mashed potatoes.

Broccoli and Cashews

2 Tbl. Minced Onion	1 Pack Cashews
1 Cup Sour Cream	2 Tbl. Butter
1 Tsp. Vinegar	½ Tsp. Poppy Seeds
½ Tsp. Paprika	2 Packs Frozen Broccoli

Cook and drain broccoli. Brown onions in butter until clear. Remove from heat. Stir in sour cream, sugar, vinegar and seasonings. Pour over broccoli and top with cashews.

Cathy's Scalloped Russet & Sweet Potatoes

2 Peeled Sweet Potatoes, sliced thin
2 Peeled Russet Potatoes, sliced thin
1 Small Diced Onion
1 Cup Warmed Half & Half
Salt & Pepper to Taste

In a buttered oval baking dish, layer all potatoes. Salt, pepper and place onion between layers, then pour half and half over the top. Microwave for 3 minutes. Cover with foil and bake at 375 degrees for one hour. Remove foil for the last thirty minutes. Done when potatoes are tender.

David Bromstad's Chocolate Chip Sea Salt Cookies

1 ¾ Cup All-Purpose Flour	1 Tsp. Baking Soda
1 Stick Unsalted Butter	1 Cup Light Brown Sugar
¼ Cup Granulated Sugar	2 Large Eggs
1 Tsp. Vanilla Extract	9 Oz. Dark Chocolate
Chips	
1 ¼ Cup Rolled Oats	
6 Tsp. Maldon or Large-Flake Sea Salt	

Whisk flour, baking soda, salt and set aside. Beat butter and sugars until fluffy, then add eggs (one at a time) beating in between, then vanilla. Add the flour mixture and beat until combined. Stir in the chocolate chips and oats until evenly distributed. Form dough into balls (about 4 Tbl. Each) and arrange 2 inches apart on baking sheets lined with parchment paper. Bake at 375 until cookies are lightly brown on edges, 15 to 18 minutes. Immediately sprinkle large-flake sea salt onto each cookie. Let cool 2 minutes before transferring to a rack to finish cooling. Makes 2 dozen.

Becky's Carrot Pecan Cake

1 ¼ Cup Salad Oil	2 Cup Sugar
2 Cups Sifted Flour	1 Tsp. Baking Powder
1 Tsp. Baking Soda	1 Tsp. Salt
1 Tbl. Cinnamon	4 Eggs
3 Cups Grated Carrots	1 Cup Finely Chopped Pecans

Combine oil and sugar, then mix well. Sift half the dry ingredients into the sugar mixture. Sift, then blend remaining ingredients, alternately with eggs, one at a time, mixing well after each addition. Add carrots and mix well. Mix in pecans then pour into a lightly oiled ten-inch tube pan or three nine inch round pans. Bake at 325 degrees for about one hour and ten minutes. Cool, then remove from pan. Split into three layers.

Emily's Plumb Wonderful Cake

1 ½ Cup Sugar	1 Cup Buttermilk
1 Cup Oil	2 Cups Self-Rising Flour
3 Eggs	1 Tsp. Baking Soda
1 Cup Pureed Prunes	1 Tsp. Cinnamon
1 Tsp. Nutmeg	1 Tsp. Allspice
1 Cup Chopped Nuts	1 Cup Raisins

After pureeing prunes and raisins in blender or food processor, mix all ingredients and bake in a Bundt pan at 350 degrees for 40 to 45 minutes. Drizzle topping over warm cake. (It is as wonderful as the carrot cake, only more moist—yum!)

Prune Cake Topping:

1 Cup Sugar	½ Cup Buttermilk

¼ Cup Butter (1/2 stick)   1 Tsp. Nutmeg
1 Tsp. Vanilla

Mix and stir in saucepan until brought to a boil. Boil for five minutes. Pour over warm cake.

COMING ATTRACTIONS, SEQUELS OR SEQUINS? YOU DECIDE!

DON'T GET YOUR UNDIES IN A BUNCH, early 2019.

This book shows you how much fun you can have regardless of your age. It contains more recipes, wisdom and outrageous true life adventures.

DECORATING ISN'T A JOKE OR IS IT? Follows in late 2019!

49010856R00133

Made in the USA
Columbia, SC
18 January 2019